UNDERSTANDING

EQUINE LAW

YOUR **GUIDE** TO HORSE HEALTH
CARE AND MANAGEMENT

D0838789

ISBN 1-58150-037-8

Printed in the United States of America

First Edition: September 1999

1 2 3 4 5 6 7 8 9 10

UNDERSTANDING

EQUINE LAW

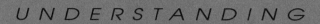

YOUR **GUIDE** TO HORSE HEALTH
CARE AND MANAGEMENT

By Milton C. Toby and Karen L. Perch, Ph.D.

The Blood-Horse, Inc. Lexington, KY

Contents

INTRODUCTION

Despite the title of this book, "equine law" really doesn't exist as a separate area for the practice of law. Attorneys who focus their clientele on horse owners, and would-be horse owners, use a combination of several specific areas of the law. Such attorneys use portions of the law related to business formation to help people select the proper form of ownership for a business involving horses. Tax law has a bearing on the form of business ownership, deductions for expenses, depreciation, estate planning, etc., that horse owners may need to know. Attorneys use principles of contract law to describe fully an agreement between two or more persons or entities, whether it's an agreement to buy or sell, to breed, or to board a horse. Whether you are in an equine business, or have one horse that you consider a part of the family, you should find useful information in *Understanding Equine Law*.

When you have finished reading this book, you will not know everything there is to know about the law as it relates to your horse or your business. You will not be able to do everything for yourself without hiring an accountant and/or attorney. Because we cannot tell you anything specific about the laws of your state that could have a bearing on decisions you may need to make, we have focused on federal laws or the laws in Kentucky, where we practice, whenever specific information is provided. One of our goals in writing this is to help you identify some of the questions you should discuss with your attorney. You may not find an attorney practicing "equine law" in your community. Don't despair. An attorney who is good at tax law, for example, can help you with tax questions related to your equine business. One who does estate planning can help you plan for care of a beloved member of the family, your horse, in the event something should happen to you. None of this means that you will need an army of attorneys. You should not, however, attempt to rely on this publication as your sole source of legal advice. This text is not intended to provide any specific legal advice to any reader. Instead, readers should find this text helpful in identifying some of the important questions to be asked of their own legal advisers.

To help address some of the issues you might face, we have invented the completely fictional family of Peter and Mary Green. Peter and Mary have two children, John and Amy. The Greens are U.S. citizens. They have never been clients of ours. If they happen to resemble any living person or group, this is purely coincidental. You'll learn more about the Greens as you proceed through the chapters of this book. You will also learn from their questions, and perhaps even their mistakes, some of the issues that you may need to consider in your own ventures.

Milton C. Toby, J.D.
Karen L. Perch, Ph.D., J.D.
Attorneys at Law
Lexington, Kentucky

CHAPTER 1

Ways to Own an Equine Business

The Greens have two pleasure horses of their own and extra room in their barn. They would like to board a few horses to help cover some of their own expenses and maybe to make some extra money. On their 300-acre family-owned farm in the Midwest, they have several riding trails. Mr. and Mrs. Green would like to make some of the trails available to riders. They don't want to pay any more in taxes than necessary, and they want to protect themselves from liability if riders are injured using the trails. The Greens know that there are many kinds of businesses but they don't know the differences between the forms of ownership. Nor do the Greens know all their ownership options, or what to consider in choosing a form of ownership. As you will see, no single form of ownership will be best for all situations.

GOING IT ALONE

Either Mr. or Mrs. Green can run their equine business as a sole proprietor. In that case, the business will have no separate identity and will not be subject to taxation as an entity. The sole proprietor will simply report all income and losses on Schedule C of the Form 1040 federal income tax returns. The greatest advantages of this method of doing business include the simplicity and the freedom to make all managerial decisions. However, the sole proprietor will be fully and personally liable for all debts of the equine business, and any other liabilities of the business. By being a sole owner, he or she could incur personal liability for personal injuries to riders, to horses, and to employees caring for the horses and maintaining the trails, to mention just a few. This major disadvantage often leads individuals to seek some other form of ownership for the business.

> ## AT A GLANCE
>
> • There are several different forms of business ownership from which to choose.
>
> • Each form of ownership has advantages and disadvantages.
>
> • Be aware of tax and insurance issues that could affect your business.
>
> • Do your homework before consulting advisers.

CORPORATE AND PARTNERSHIP OPTIONS MAKE ALPHABET SOUP

If the Greens want something other than a sole proprietorship, they will have to get into the world of corporations and partnerships. Each form has advantages and disadvantages.

Should the Greens incorporate their equine business? Good question. The answer depends on what Peter and Mary Green want to accomplish. Several forms of ownership are available to them. Incorporating a business means creating a separate legal entity of the business, complete with all the legal characteristics of any corporation. A corporation can be either a "C" corporation or an "S" corporation.

THE C CORPORATION

The C corporation has investor shareholders, with its own legal identity. It generally can continue to exist beyond the lifetime of any individual investor. One advantage of the C corporation is the possibility of an unlimited number of investors. Another is the corporation's ability to issue more than one class of stock, so that some shareholders may earn dividends and others may not. The most important advantage of a C corporation is probably the limited liability of the shareholders. An investor in such a corporation will risk the loss of his or her personal investment in the company but, under ordinary circumstances, an investor would not be liable for the debts of the corporation itself.

The biggest disadvantage for most owners of small businesses is probably the federal income tax treatment. Corporations are taxpayers, just like individuals. This means that if the Greens decide to incorporate their business, the corporation will pay its own income taxes out of its earnings. If the corporation pays dividends on the shares held by the Greens, the Greens will pay taxes on the earnings distributed to them. If the corporation pays the Greens for the work they do in the business, the corporation will have an income tax deduction for the wages paid to the Greens. But the Greens will pay income taxes on their earnings as employees of the corporation. Because there are now corporate income taxes to pay, if the equine business is incorporated, it will have to earn more money than before incorporation if the Greens are to have the same amount of money available to spend.

THE S CORPORATION

Like a C corporation, an S corporation can have more than one investor. This form of corporation has very strict technical requirements. Procedurally, the shareholders of a C corporation can elect to have Subchapter S status under the Internal Revenue Code *if* the C corporation applies within a specified period of time and meets all other requirements. Some of these include a limit on the number of shareholders, who must be individuals, estates, or certain qualified trusts.

Shareholders cannot be nonresident aliens and the S corporation cannot have more than one class of stock. Although the IRS will limit the number of shareholders to no more than 35, for purposes of counting, husbands and wives count as one shareholder. If the Greens decide to form a corporation, they can form a C corporation and then apply for tax treatment under Subchapter S of the Internal Revenue Code. A major advantage of the S Corporation status for the Greens would be that the corporation would not be taxed at the entity level. Instead, income and losses of the corporation would be passed on to the Greens on their individual tax returns. Their two children can own shares in the business, which could be helpful in ensuring a smooth, uninterrupted continuation of the equine business following the deaths of Peter and Mary. For some, the technical requirements are the biggest disadvantage of this form of ownership.

THE GENERAL PARTNERSHIP (GP)

The Greens could operate their business as a partnership, if they want. Several forms of partnerships exist, three of which are discussed in this chapter. A general partnership, where at least two individuals join together in a business enterprise, is one option. The general partnership will file its own tax returns reporting income and expenses on federal income tax Form 1065. All gains and losses flow through to the partners and are treated, for tax purposes, in much the same way as a sole proprietorship. Like the sole proprietorship, the general partnership is simpler than either type of corporation. Also like the sole proprietorship, the partners are personally liable for the debts and other liabilities of the business. In addition, all general partners can be held liable for business actions or omissions of the other partners.

THE LIMITED PARTNERSHIP (LP)

A limited partnership is also a possibility. In that case, the Greens must have at least one general partner, who would have primary decision-making power for the operation of the business. All general partners can be held liable for the debts and liabilities of the business, as well as for the acts or omissions of the other general partners. The limited partnership, however, has an important advantage for limited partners. They will be liable for losses of the firm only to the extent of their investment, a feature of this business entity that is similar to that of a C corporation. Limited partners do not participate in management and cannot permit their names to be used by the limited partnership. If they do, they may lose their status as limited partners.

A disadvantage of this form of business ownership can result from the fact that the limited partners turn over decision-making responsibility to the general managers. In years when there are business losses, the loss is treated as a passive loss which, for tax purposes, can be offset only against passive income. The limited partnership generally requires a partnership agreement, the requirements of which may vary from state to state.

Occasionally, a limited partnership may be treated as a corporation for tax purposes, because the ownership interests of the limited partners are so similar to that of shareholders in a corporation. The Greens probably won't get the protections they want with this form of ownership, based on what they describe as their needs.

At least two other forms of ownership may be available to the Greens for their business. Two will be briefly discussed here. One is the limited liability company. The other is the limited liability partnership.

THE LIMITED LIABILITY COMPANY (LLC)

Like a partnership, the limited liability company passes income and losses through to the partners. All partners receive this tax treatment, even those that participate in the active management of the business. In states that allow this form of ownership, the tax and other reporting requirements may be less complex. As of this writing, the limited liability company is not recognized in every state. The Greens should consult both their financial and legal advisers to determine if this form of ownership is available in their state. They also need to know how they should form such a company in order to allow the income and losses to pass through to the individual owners of the company. Under some circumstances, the company may be treated for tax purposes as a C corporation. One disadvantage of this form of ownership for Peter and Mary is that it is very difficult to transfer or sell ownership interests in this form of company.

Because it is a somewhat newer form of business than those previously discussed, the body of law regarding the legal and working relationships within the company is comparatively small. The same is true with respect to case law regarding the extent to which the individuals can be held liable for actions of the managers. In addition, this form of ownership is not yet recognized in all 50 states. Therefore, before choosing this form of ownership, the Greens would have to make sure that it is recognized in any other state in which they may want to transact business. If not, there is no real way to know how such a state might treat non-managers with respect to actions taken by the managers.

THE LIMITED LIABILITY PARTNERSHIP (LLP)

Although this is a form of partnership, it is mentioned here, rather than with the discussions of general and limited partnerships, because this form of ownership is also fairly new. Like the limited liability company, it may not be recognized in every state. In those states that do recognize the limited liability partnership, its characteristics are similar to those of a general partnership, except that the individual partners are not held personally liable for the actions of the other partners. The partner who incurs the expense, debt, or other liability will be held liable for any acts or omissions that in any way harm the business.

Tax treatment is similar to that of general partnerships, with income and losses passing through to the partners. Partners also are free to actively participate in management. On the other hand, the administrative requirements tend to be more complex and cumbersome than those of a general partnership. This form of ownership also may suffer from a

limited body of case law. In addition, if a limited liability partnership transacts business outside the state in which it is
formed, any agreement limiting the liability of individuals
may not be honored, especially if the second state does not
recognize this form of ownership.

The Greens want to minimize their potential for personal
liability for accidents, injuries, and so forth. It should be
obvious that they can select a form of ownership for the business that will provide a measure of protection for personal
assets, but that they cannot protect the assets of the business
from such liabilities.

THE GOVERNMENT WANTS ITS MONEY!

By now, it should be apparent that we don't know enough
about the particular circumstances to advise the Greens on
the best form of ownership. They've told us that they want
to board horses and to open up some of the trails on their
land to riders. We know that they don't want to pay any
more taxes than necessary and that they want to protect
themselves from various liabilities as much as possible. They
still need additional information about some very basic tax
issues that will apply to their business. Information about insurance also will help. State tax liability, a subject beyond the
scope of this book, also should be considered.

HOBBY LOSSES — YOU CAN'T HAVE TOO MUCH FUN

The Internal Revenue Service carefully examines new small
business returns for compliance with its "hobby loss" rules.
The less formal the form of ownership, the more likely it is
that the Internal Revenue Service will scrutinize the business
to determine if it is a real business, rather than just a hobby.
The hobby loss rules exist to prevent individuals from claiming tax deductions on business losses for something that is
not really a business, such as a hobby. At the outset, the taxpayer has the burden to prove that it intends to make a profit
with its business. It is not necessary that the business actual-

ly always shows a profit, however. If the Greens can show a profit in at least two out of any seven consecutive years, including the first year of business loss, they will gain the presumption that they intend to make a profit from their business. Once they have made the required showing of profit intent, the burden will shift to the Internal Revenue Service to disprove the Greens' intent to make a profit. The Greens can enjoy the business they want to have, but they also must work at it.

The Internal Revenue Service examines several other aspects of the business to determine if an activity is really a business, or just a hobby in disguise. Other factors considered include the taxpayer's knowledge about the details of the business, whether the taxpayer consults with other experts for business advice, the amount of time and effort the taxpayer spends on the activity, the existence of recreational aspects of the business from the taxpayer's point of view, and the expectation, if any, for appreciation of business assets.

During the period in which they attempt to establish profit intent, and forever thereafter, the Greens must organize their record keeping, regardless of the form of ownership they select. They also must stay informed, even if they hire others to do some parts of the work. They should consult with appropriate legal and financial advisers, as well as with any other expert who could provide business advice. The people who ride the trails on the Greens' land can have all the recreation they want. The Greens have to work while they ride their trails and feed their horses. And if they keep careful records, they can show both federal and state taxing authorities that they have a legitimate boarding and trail riding business.

PASSIVE LOSSES — YOU HAVE TO REALLY WORK AT THE BUSINESS

Not only will the Internal Revenue Service want to make sure that the Greens don't have too much fun, it also will want to take an extra look at the business to make sure that they really are working at the business — and not just hiring someone else to do everything, with no involvement on their part. This is where the passive loss rules come into play. For example, suppose the Greens suffer a passive loss as a result of the boarding of horses. They want to be able to deduct these losses from their other earned income. In order to do so, they will have to be able to convince the Internal Revenue Service that they have materially participated in the business. In plain English, the Greens can establish material participation by showing that at least one of them spent more than 500 hours in the business in which the loss was incurred, during the taxable year of the loss. As husband and wife, they will be allowed to combine their efforts to meet this rule. If they cannot meet the 500 hour requirement, they can try to satisfy a 100-hour provision. If they spend, together, at least 100 hours throughout the tax year in which the loss was incurred, and if they can show that they actively participated on a regular basis throughout the tax year, they may be able to deduct the losses from boarding horses against other earned income.

If the Greens cannot meet either of these tests, they will only be able to deduct the losses against other passive income, such as investment income. The Greens need to keep these rules in mind as they decide the form of ownership that might be best for their horse business. They also might want to know that present federal tax rules would allow them to deduct all losses that they were previously disallowed, because of lack of material participation, should they at some point decide to sell the business. During the year of the sale they would be able to claim any earlier disallowed passive losses.

TAX ISSUE: SCHEDULE C OR SCHEDULE F

Up to now, the Greens have probably reported their farm income and losses on Schedule F of the Federal Form 1040. If they operate the equine business as an entity separate from the farm, they will have to file Schedule C, as well. Other forms also could be required. This should not be a factor in their decision-making about form of ownership for the business. Rather, it is simply a matter of which they should be aware as they talk to their financial advisers.

TIMING IS EVERYTHING

The Greens have not told us whether they intend to place any of their own horses in service for the trail riding portion of their business. If they do, they need to be familiar with the federal tax regulations pertaining to horses as business assets. For depreciation purposes, age is determined by the actual date of birth of the horse. (For most purposes, a horse becomes a year older on January 1, regardless of the animal's actual birthday.) As a general rule, unless a horse is over 12 years old and used for breeding, or over two years old and used as a racehorse, the depreciation period will be seven years. Horses in the two categories just mentioned will be depreciated over three years. The Greens can elect to use a longer depreciation period than the seven years their horses would probably have. It also matters to the Internal Revenue Service when, during the tax year, the horse is placed in service for the trail riding business. If the Greens begin their business too late in the year, they will not be allowed to take a full year's deduction.

INSURANCE

The Greens can provide themselves with a measure of protection from liability, regardless of the form of business ownership they select, by purchasing a general liability insurance policy. Sometimes these may be known as umbrella policies, and are separate from their property insurance. It can protect them against losses from any damage, accident, injury, etc., to people or property, caused in some way by their own horses. Under some circumstances, they may be able to buy insurance to protect themselves from death of a horse in their care from occurrences that we generally consider "acts of God," such as lightning and fire. They may not find a source of separate insurance coverage to protect them from liabilities caused by them or their employees in negligently caring for the horses boarded with them. It might be possible for this to be covered under their general business liability policy.

DO YOUR HOMEWORK!

It is probably obvious by now that the Greens have not provided us with enough information to really be able to tell them everything they need to know to get started. At this point, it is not apparent that they have even considered some of the things an adviser would need to know. Now it's our turn to give them a list of things to think about or do before coming back. As you read through the list, you will realize that they will not have all the answers at their fingertips. Nor will the Greens have enough personal knowledge of every subject to develop answers to every question even after careful thought. They will have to consult various advisers in areas where they lack knowledge or understanding.

If you are interested in starting an equine business of some type, the forms of ownership, tax, and insurance issues we've discussed may help you in reaching some decisions. You, too, however, should think about the following list of questions. These are the sorts of things that belong in a business plan. We realize that even this list may not be complete, but you should use it to guide you in writing your own business plan.

WRITE IT ALL DOWN

1. Is your entire property located within the borders of one state? If not, you may need to take into account the laws of multiple jurisdictions in planning your business.

2. Who owns the business? [In the Greens' case, is it Peter? Mary? Both? As tenants in common? As joint tenants with (or without) right of survivorship? As tenants by the entirety?]

3. In what state(s) do you intend to do business of some kind?

4. How many people do you want making day to day management decisions? Who would you prefer to have making those decisions?

5. How much hands-on participation do you, and others who may invest or join in the business with you, want to have in the business? Does that vary at all according to the tasks being considered? For example, is one or the other more interested in, or suited for, leading trail rides? Physical care of the horses? Financial record-keeping? Communicating with the public about the business?

6. Are your children, if any, adults? Do you want your children to participate in the business? Do the children want to participate in the business?

7. Have you identified anyone else with a similar business from whom you might be able to gain advice (preferably not a direct competitor)? Have you actually consulted such a person?

8. Will adding this business to your existing farm operation require an initial investment of capital on your part? How much can you afford to invest initially in this new business?

9. What are your long-term goals for the business and for yourself personally? Do you and the relevant others share the same goals? Have you talked about these things, or have you just assumed that they have the same goals? Are the goals attainable? Do they also provide some measure of challenge?

10. How risk averse are you and any relevant others, such as your spouse, investors, etc.? Do you agree on the amount and types of business risk you are willing to accept?

11. Do you have an actual business plan? If so,

      a) Is it in writing?

      b) Does it identify the business goals and objectives? The purpose of the business?

      c) Does it identify the form of business entity? Is the

business form you've chosen one that is allowed in your state? Have you spoken to any advisers about this yet?

d) Does it list types of advisers to consult?

e) Does it explain where you will obtain the initial capital needed to begin the investment? Does it state how much capital you need to invest?

f) Does it identify how you will find and secure the business of clients wanting to board horses with you? Does it explain how, where, and how often you will advertise the availability of trails for pleasure riding (or whatever you are doing in your equine business)?

g) Does it give you a time-line of some sort, so you can compare your intended progress to your actual progress?

h) Does it estimate projected income and expenditures for the next year? Two years? Three years?

i) Does it specify how long the business will last? Common choices are "in perpetuity," meaning the business will continue indefinitely, or "for a term of (x) years," such as 10 or 20.

12. Have you established a business relationship with a veterinarian? Will that person be available on a regular basis to provide medical care for horses?

13. Have you opened a separate bank account for the new business?

14. Have you applied for the appropriate federal employer identification number (EIN) for the new business? Do you already have an EIN for the farm operation?

15. Have you applied for account numbers with any relevant state and local taxing authorities?

16. Will the added business affect in any way your obligation to participate in federal and/or state unemployment or worker's compensation programs?

17. Have you obtained or developed a satisfactory method or system for keeping track of the time you spend on the business, as well as the revenue and expenses?

18. Do you have any plans to expand the scope of your

horse business in the future? For example, do you anticipate getting into areas such as breeding or racing? If you anticipate getting into breeding, have you considered the market you want to reach? Are you talking about breeding horses for pleasure riding or ranching, or to race?

19. If you have considered getting into the business of racing horses, how will you acquire such horses? Do you understand the mechanics of claiming race purchases in your state? Do you know how auctions work? At this point, have you considered the possibility of joining or forming a partnership for the specific purpose of buying a share of a racehorse?

20. Are you familiar with the concept of syndicates, in which you can participate as co-owners with others by contractual agreement as to capital to be raised, the interests in the specific horse to be sold, method of decision-making, responsibility for income, expenses, and tax consequences, and liability of investors (which is unlimited)?

It will be a lot of work for the Greens to answer all these questions. It will be even more work to put it all on paper. But that is exactly what they should do. In this way they can make sensible choices as they implement their business — whether they are thinking about how they will own their business, who will do the work, how they will find customers, or what will happen to the business when they are gone. If you want to begin an equine business of some sort, you, too, should think about your goals and concerns as you answer the same kinds of questions you read here. You can take these answers to your financial and legal advisers, who will be in a much better position to help than if you simply walked in and said, "I want to start boarding horses on my farm."

CHAPTER 2

Contracts

If you take away only one thing from reading this book, it should be this: Get it in writing!

Horse business traditionally has been conducted with nothing more than the strength of a handshake binding the parties. That was never sound business practice, and the following rule of thumb should govern your business dealings: If a particular outcome to a business transaction is important (getting to breed your mare to a certain stallion, for example), or if the effect of an unexpected problem would be unacceptable (such as a costly injury to a boarder or her horse), you should insist on a written contract with the other party.

The Greens, like most people in the horse industry today, conduct their equine activities without resorting to written contracts. They sometimes enter into oral agreements with feed and equipment dealers, boarders, and riders using their land, and these oral agreements are occasionally comprehensive enough to protect the Greens. More often than not, though, the Greens trust their business and personal fortunes to a shaky combination of faith that others will do the right thing, and a fervent hope that nothing will go wrong. Usually, they are right.

The Greens' objections to using and requiring written contracts should sound familiar to everyone: "It is too much trouble to use a written contract." "No one else around here does it that way." "I don't know how to write a contract and lawyers are too expensive anyway." "My customers will think that I don't trust them if I make them sign a contract before I board their horse, or before I let them ride on my land." "My boarders will go to another farm where they don't have to sign a contract." "I don't want to make the feed supplier mad."

These are all legitimate concerns, particularly if, like the Greens, you are operating a small horse business on a shoestring. No one wants to add complication and aggravation to a business or pleasure activity, and many horse enthusiasts view the use of written contracts as far more hassle than benefit. After all, you may think, nothing bad has happened yet. What is the worst thing that can happen to me if I continue to do business as usual, without written agreements with my customers?

For starters, you might be responsible for a hefty veterinarian bill that a reluctant client refuses to pay, or you might have to absorb unpaid board bills with no legal recourse, or you might face lawsuits arising from a variety of situations.

Using written contracts will not protect you from everything that might go wrong, of course; nothing can do that. Proper use of well-drafted written contracts can allow you to predict the outcome when something unexpected happens, and that is the real value of getting agreements in writing. You might enjoy a surprise treat on your birthday, but the fewer surprises you have to face where your farm and horses

AT A GLANCE

- Get it in writing! Insist on written contracts.

- Written contracts allow you to predict the outcome when something unexpected happens.

- A contract's terms should be tailored to the transaction's individual circumstances.

- One of the most important clauses in a boarding contract deals with emergency care authorization.

- Boarding contracts should have a "hold harmless" clause for the farm's protection.

are concerned, the better off you are.

A contract is nothing more than a set of promises between the parties, a promise by one person to do something in return for a second person's promise to do something else. A valid contract can be either written or oral, although, as will be seen later, written is better. A contract can be as simple as an agreement between two people outlined on a cocktail napkin, or as complicated as a multi-page, multi-party document crammed to the four corners with incomprehensible fine-print legalese. A valid contract creates legal obligations between the parties, and allows for enforcement in court if the contract is broken.

The value of a valid, enforceable contract is that it allows the parties to avoid surprise in the event a business transaction does not go as planned. While even a professionally-drafted contract cannot anticipate every potential problem, a well-drafted contract should cover the problems most likely to occur. The Greens almost learned this lesson the hard way.

The Greens have been involved in the horse business for several years, as competitors at local shows, as horse owners, and as small-scale breeders. They presently own two horses, which they keep on their farm a few miles from town. One of Mrs. Green's co-workers, a secretary, just bought her first horse, a gelding intended for trail riding, and she wants to board the animal at the Greens' farm. She will be the first client for the Greens' boarding business. Obviously, the extra money will come in handy.

The Greens and their new boarder come to a mutual understanding. After a lengthy chat on the telephone, the new boarder agrees that while the horse is at the Greens' farm, she will be responsible for several specific expenses: board, including feed and a safe stall; veterinary care; and farrier services. The Greens agree to notify the horse's owner before incurring any non-emergency expenses.

The Greens and the boarder have entered into an oral contract. The Greens have promised to provide certain boarding services, for which the owner has promised to pay. Their boarder also has agreed to pay for specific out-of-pocket expenses. As we will see, there also are several other important terms that the Greens and their boarder have not covered.

A few months later, while making a final check of the barn before turning in for the evening, Mrs. Green notices that the new horse is showing some signs of colic. He appears nervous and he is sweating and nipping at his flanks. The situation does not appear critical, though, and Mrs. Green attempts to contact the horse's owner before calling the veterinarian.

The owner is not available, however, and the horse's condition appears to worsen. Mr. Green contacts their regular veterinarian, who comes to the farm for an after-hours emergency call. He diagnoses the condition as a potentially serious colic, and recommends immediate surgery. Still unable to contact the horse's owner, the Greens authorize the surgery, which saves the animal's life. The bill for the surgery and postoperative care amounts to several thousand dollars, which the veterinarian bills directly to the horse's owner at Mr. Green's instruction.

At this point, one of two things will happen. The owner pays the veterinarian bill (either with or without attendant grumbling), or she refuses. If the owner does not pay the bill, the veterinarian looks to the Greens (who authorized the surgery) for payment. The ultimate outcome may rest on the fact that the Greens and their boarder never executed a written boarding contract.

This common situation illustrates two important points about contracts. First, if everything goes as expected — the Greens incur unauthorized expenses on behalf of the owner in an emergency, and the boarder pays the bill when it arrives — a contract will have no practical impact. Because the expectations of both parties were satisfied, neither party should have any complaints. In other words, although neither party anticipated the problem, the outcome surprises no one.

If, on the other hand, one of the parties fails to perform as promised, the value of a contract becomes obvious. Consider, for example, what happens if the Greens' boarder balks at paying what she calls a "ridiculous" veterinarian bill for unnecessary and unauthorized surgery, a likely reaction from a first-time horse owner with limited disposable income. The veterinarian, naturally, looks to the Greens for payment, since they authorized the surgical procedure in the first place. They pay the bill to preserve a good relationship with the veterinarian, who happens to be the only veterinarian with equine expertise within 50 miles, then seek reimbursement from the boarder. If the boarder balks at reimbursing the Greens, their only recourse for getting paid is to take the boarder to court.

The oral boarding agreement between the Greens and the owner sets out some, but not all, of the responsibilities and obligations of both parties. In this example, the Greens have a responsibility to attempt to notify the owner in a non-emergency situation and the boarder has an obligation to pay the veterinarian's bill. When the Greens go to court in an attempt to force the owner to reimburse them for the bill, the judge or jury will have some basis for allocating the cost of the surgery. Here, the terms of the contract show that the owner of the horse is responsible for the veterinarian bill. Without an agreement of some kind, however, the Greens' chances of forcing the reluctant owner to pay are small.

This leads to the second important principle regarding contracts. While any contract is better than no contract, a written contract is better. In the example above, the boarding agreement should be valid and enforceable, though it was an oral agreement between the Greens and the horse owner.

Having an agreement memorialized in writing and signed by the parties does not guarantee that the parties will abide by the agreement. The advantage of a written contract is that neither the existence of the contract nor its terms is in doubt. In the case of an oral contract, however, the first step to enforcing the agreement in court often involves simply proving that the contract actually existed, and if it did exist, that the terms of the agreement are as you claim. This can be a difficult task when, months or years after the fact, memories have faded and interests may have changed. No matter how reasonable the Greens' actions in the above example were, they may find themselves on the paying end of a large veterinarian bill for someone else's horse if they must rely on an oral agreement to prove that the owner really is responsible for the emergency care they authorized for her.

There is no such thing as a "one size fits all" contract. Each contract represents a particular business transaction, and the terms of the contract should be tailored to the transaction's individual circumstances. A properly drafted boarding contract should address different concerns than a contract for leasing a competition horse, for example, and the respective contracts should be drafted with the particular transaction in mind. This does not mean that you cannot have a standard contract for boarding, or leasing, or for lessons; you can, and should, have standard contracts for common situations. You must be mindful that even a comprehensive standard contract may have to be modified to fit a particular situation.

CONTRACTS 101

The Greens were lucky. Their first experience with a boarder could have cost them several thousand dollars, and a friend, if the boarder had decided to back out of the oral agreement. To avoid such problems in the future, they decide to use written contracts with their boarders. Every boarding contract should include several elements, and you should be familiar with them, whether you are working with your attorney in drafting a contract, attempting to customize a generic fill-in-the-blanks contract from a book (something we do not advise), or simply considering whether to sign a contract prepared by someone else.

Boarding contracts generally are prepared by, and for the benefit of, farm owners, but this is not always the case. Many boarding farms do not use written contracts, and in those situations it is the responsibility of the horse owner to insist on a written contract. You, as a boarder, have a right to be protected by a written agreement, and you can, and should, insist on one. If the boarding establishment does not have a written contract, you should be prepared to offer a contract of your own.

Besides using written contracts when they board horses for others, the Greens should require written agreements when they allow others to use their land for trail riding, when they sell or buy horses, when they lease a horse, and when they send a mare to a stallion for breeding. They also should consider written contracts when purchasing large quantities of hay and grain, tack (at least from private individuals), and farm equipment.

IDENTIFY THE PARTIES

Every contract should identify by name, address, and contact telephone number the persons or businesses that are parties to the agreement. If one, or both, of the parties is a business, the contract also should include a statement that the person executing the contract actually has authority to act for the business he or she represents. All parties to the contract should sign and date it.

IDENTIFY THE HORSE

Anytime a horse is the subject of a contract, whether for boarding, leasing, sale or purchase, or breeding, the written agreement should clearly identify the animal. The reasons for this requirement should be obvious, because misidentifications can, and do, happen. The description should be sufficient to easily identify the horse in question, and should include color, markings, breed, sex, age, any registration number tattoos or freeze brands, and scars or other distinctive points. A photograph can be attached to the contract, and can make it easier to separate one "bay, no white" from another.

It also is important to record in detail the animal's physical condition, and any indications of previous injury. This should be done before you assume responsibility for the animal, for the same reason that prudent customers carefully examine a rental car for dents and scratches and report them to the rental agent before driving the car away from the rental lot.

Any tack or other equipment accompanying the horse also should be listed and identified to avoid later disputes about ownership of those items.

WHO PAYS WHAT, WHEN, AND HOW MUCH?

Board charges can be calculated on a "per day" or "per month" basis. The latter is more common, because the monthly bill is not dependent on the number of days in the month and less bookkeeping is required. "Per day" charges, on the other hand, make it easier to pro rate a bill for a boarder who arrives or leaves in the middle of a month.

The contract should show when the farm will provide a bill to the boarder (every month is standard), and when the boarder must pay the bill. A board bill usually becomes due on the first of every month, with a grace period of a few days before the bill becomes overdue. For the farm's protection, the contract should include a provision allowing the farm to charge interest on overdue bills. The interest rate, such as 1.5% per month, also should be stated.

The contract should specify which out-of-pocket expenses are the responsibility of the owner. In the Greens' example above, the owner assumed responsibility for farrier and veterinary services. For show horses, out-of-pocket expenses might include transportation to shows, instruction at the show grounds, and grooming and braiding charges. Whether out-of-pocket expenses will be paid by the farm and then billed to the owner, or billed directly to the owner by the person providing the service, also should be stated in the contract. The latter is more convenient for the farm owner, but a supplier might prefer to bill the farm rather than risk non-payment from an unknown horse owner.

Finally, the contract should explain the nature of each bill. For example, the bill due on May 1 could include the board charges for the coming month (requiring a boarder to pay in advance protects the farm), plus any out-of-pocket expenses that were incurred during the preceding month.

Many boarding contracts include the phrase "In consideration of $_____ ..." or similar language. In this context, "consideration" is a legal concept that refers to the money paid by the boarder to the farm owner. It represents the inducement for the farm owner to provide the promised boarding services. Consideration of some kind is necessary for a valid contract.

WHAT DO I GET FOR MY MONEY?

The contract should state that the farm will provide normal and reasonable care, and explain in detail the services and facilities that the farm is agreeing to provide as part of the board. These can include stall or pasture board, turn-out service, exercise, grooming, training, and anything else about which the parties can agree. Whether you are the farm owner or the boarder, it is important to understand what will, and will not, be provided. Any special instructions relating to the horse's care also should be explained in detail.

THE EXCULPATORY CLAUSE

Most attorneys recommend including in boarding contracts an exculpatory clause in which the boarder agrees to a waiver of the farm's liability for personal injuries or injuries to the horse. This is important because of the nature of a boarding transaction. When one party (here the horse owner, or bailor) delivers property to another (the farm owner, or bailee), they create a bailment. A bailment generally does not create a fiduciary relationship between the parties, such as that of a trustee or guardian, in which a duty to act for the benefit of the horse owner would be imposed by law on the owner of the farm. A bailment does impose upon the person accepting the property (the farm owner) the duty to exercise ordinary care.

The common law rule is that when a bailment is created, the farm owner into whose care the boarding horse is entrusted is presumed to be responsible for any harm suffered by the horse. If a lawsuit arises, the presumption that the farm was at fault can be overcome by evidence that, more likely than not, the farm exercised ordinary care. A few states, like Kentucky, have adopted statutes that shift the responsibility for loss to the owner of a boarded horse, and in recent years many states have imposed limitations on liability (often for personal injury) for harm suffered while engaging in equine activities. Equine liability laws are discussed in general in a later chapter of this book; an attorney familiar with the laws of your state can advise you whether such statutes should affect the decision to include an exculpatory clause in your boarding contract.

There is no required wording for an exculpatory clause, unless the laws of your state require it. The parties should agree that while the contract is in force, the horse owner assumes all risk of loss for the animal. The boarder also should agree to hold the farm harmless for any and all injuries to the horse. Whatever the wording, a farm owner generally cannot eliminate through contractual agreement his or her liability for negligence.

Depending on the state in which your farm is located, such exculpatory clauses may or may not be strictly enforceable. Exculpatory clauses can be valuable nevertheless. Your farm liability insurance carrier may require such a clause as a prerequisite for coverage, and the fact that a boarder has agreed to a waiver of liability might discourage a lawsuit.

CALL 911!

Horses have a peculiar affinity for getting sick or hurt, and, paradoxically, emergencies in the horse business can become almost routine. One of the most important clauses in a boarding contract deals with authorization for emergency veterinary care, both for the physical welfare of the horse and the economic welfare of the parties.

The farm owner obviously should attempt to contact the horse's owner before authorizing major veterinary procedures, but if the owner is out of reach, the contract should give the farm authority both to contact a veterinarian on the owner's behalf and to authorize appropriate veterinary care. If the boarder wishes to use a veterinarian other than one routinely employed by the farm, that veterinarian should be identified in the contract, and contact numbers should be provided by the boarder.

The farm owner and boarder also should agree on how they will pay the bill for emergency care. Will the farm owner pay, then bill the boarder, for example, or should the bill go directly to the horse owner?

ARE YOU INSURED?

Most horses are not insured. If an animal is covered by mortality or loss of use insurance, the owner in the boarding contract should note that fact. Most insurance carriers require that the company be notified when an insured animal is injured or dies, and the contract should state whether the farm has a responsibility to notify the insurance company.

A statement that the farm does not carry insurance covering boarding horses (as is usually the case), and that the owner of the horse understands and agrees to board the animal under those circumstances also should be included in the contract.

A SECURITY INTEREST

Dealing with unpaid bills for board and out-of-pocket expenses is one of the most frustrating tasks for the owner of a boarding farm and, like the question of liability, warrants a separate chapter in this book. An obvious remedy, selling the horse to recover the bill, is easier if the boarding contract includes a provision granting the farm a security interest in the horse. The contract should state that the farm has a secured interest in the horse to guarantee payment for services provided by the farm and for unpaid out-of-pocket expenses, and that the farm may sell the horse, either at a public auction or privately, to recover the unpaid balance.

The contract also should say how long an overdue bill must be delinquent before the farm owner can resort to self-help. If the horse must be sold, and the sale price obtained is greater than the amount owed, any excess generally must be returned to the horse's now former owner.

Many states have statutes that give a farm owner a security interest in a boarded horse when bills are not paid, and many farm owners prefer to rely on these agister's liens rather than ask for a security interest in a boarding contract. (Agister is legalese for a person who boards livestock.) While statutory liens can be helpful, the procedures that must be followed are complicated and generally require the farm owner to file a lawsuit, win a judgment, then proceed against the owner of the horse as a judgment creditor. The contract also should include a provision allowing the farm to recover attorney fees in the event legal assistance is required to recover a delinquent bill.

Obtaining a security interest through the boarding contract simplifies matters for the farm owner should a board bill go unpaid. If you choose to include a security interest provision in your boarding contract, you also should require the horse owner to identify any existing liens already lodged against the horse.

HOLDING THE FARM HARMLESS

A boarding contract should include a "hold harmless" clause for the farm's protection. When executing a hold harmless clause, the owner of the horse agrees to hold the farm owner without responsibility for damage or injury caused by the horse while it is being boarded. Hold harmless provisions typically require the owner of the horse to pay any legal fees or other expenses incurred by the farm owner in defending a lawsuit based on harm caused by the boarded horse. A typical example would be a situation in which a visitor to the farm is kicked or bitten by the horse being boarded. If the injured party decides to sue the farm owner, the horse owner has agreed to be responsible for the injury, and for any legal fees that arise because of the litigation.

A hold harmless clause is not all-encompassing, however. Public policy concerns generally prevent a farm owner from contracting away liability for his or her own negligence. A hold harmless clause probably would not eliminate liability for a farm owner who negligently leaves a gate open, allowing a boarder's horse to escape to the highway and cause an accident.

IN SICKNESS AND IN HEALTH

A well-managed farm should have in place policies regarding vaccinations, deworming, and tests for equine infectious anemia for boarders. These policies should be stated in detail in the boarding contract, and proof of necessary vaccinations and tests should be required before a horse is accepted for boarding.

ALL GOOD THINGS MUST COME TO AN END

Finally, a boarding contract should anticipate a time when the parties no longer wish to be bound by its terms. The contract should require written notice at least 30 days in advance if either party intends to terminate the contract. The contract also should provide for termination if either party violates the terms of the agreement, called a "breach of contract," and the party not in breach should be allowed to recover attorney fees and court costs, if any, resulting from the default.

The Greens learned a valuable lesson. For important business transactions in the future, they probably will insist on written contracts for their own protection.

A CONTRACT IS A TWO-WAY STREET

You may notice that this chapter is written primarily from the perspective of the farm owner, and if you are a boarder, you might feel slighted. You also might feel that you must give up all your rights when you sign a boarding contract. While it is true that the vast majority of boarding contracts are drafted at the behest of the farm owner for his or her protection, it is not true that a boarder must meekly accept the contract as written. Boarding a horse is a business transaction, and like nearly all business deals, is subject to bargaining.

Principles of supply and demand govern boarding transactions, and the relative bargaining power of the parties depends in large part on the availability of other boarding options and the attractiveness of the facility in question. If there are several similar competing boarding establishments in the immediate area, the balance of bargaining power shifts to the boarder, who can pick and choose. If, on the other hand, there is only one easily accessible boarding farm, or if the trainer you want for lessons only teaches at a particular farm, the balance favors the farm owner.

No matter what the circumstances, though, it never hurts to request that the farm owner change a bothersome term in the contract. If there is something you don't like in a contract, ask that it be changed. The worst that can happen is that the farm owner will refuse. If there is a contract term that you don't understand, ask your attorney for an explanation. Never sign a contract that you don't fully understand, and never sign a contract with blank spaces that the farm owner tells you will be filled in later. Finally, inform your insurance carrier that you are boarding your horse, and find out if your homeowner's or renter's policy provides coverage for injuries to other people caused by your horse at the boarding farm. Your coverage may be affected if you sign a contract with exculpatory or "hold harmless" clauses, and you may want to have your insurance agent review the contract. Remember: a well-drafted contract protects both parties. If you feel pressured to sign a contract that you feel is unfair, and the farm owner refuses to negotiate, you might want to question whether you want to embark on a business relationship with this person.

MAJORITY RULES

The Greens would face a different problem if their new boarder was a high-school-age friend of one of their children, instead of Mrs. Green's adult co-worker. In the former case, even a properly drafted written contract might not be adequate.

Both the validity and enforceability of a contract depend, in part, on the legal ability of the parties to enter into a binding contract. This legal ability is called the "capacity to contract," and it frequently comes into play when a young person attempts to execute a contract. If the Greens agree to board a horse belonging to a 16-year-old, for example, even a properly drafted and executed written contract might not protect them if the boarder runs up a large bill, then refuses to pay. Similar problems can arise through the sale or lease of a horse to a minor, or when a minor backs out of an agreement to pay for riding lessons. Generally, when the parties to a contract are an adult and a minor, the adult will be bound by the terms of the agreement, while the minor can choose to affirm or disaffirm the contact. In the example above, the contract between the Greens and their daughter's friend is voidable at the option of the minor party.

There is no requirement that a valid contract include the ages of the persons signing the agreement, but if there is doubt about the age of one of the parties, you should request some proof that he or she is not a minor. An obvious solution is never to deal with minors, but this often is not practical for a boarding farm or riding stable. An alternate solution is to require an adult, which usually will be a parent, to be jointly liable with the minor for board bills and out-of-pocket expenses. Such a provision easily can be added to a boarding contract. In most states, a minor reaches the age of majority (legal age) when he or she turns 18, but you should check the law in your particular jurisdiction.

THE MATCH GAME

This chapter deals primarily with boarding contracts, in part because a boarding transaction is one of the most common business deals in the horse business, and in part because a boarding contract is a good example of many basic elements of contract construction. Contracts should be utilized in many different situations, some of which are discussed in other parts of this book. Form of ownership, liability issues, getting paid for your services, and sales and leases, are obvious issues that can be addressed through an agreement in writing.

Other business transactions that can, and should, be memorialized in writing include shared ownership of competition or breeding animals, foal sharing, stallion syndication agreements, insurance transactions, and a variety of service agreements. A contract, in the most basic terms, is an agreement between parties that creates obligations either to do, or not to do, certain things. To be effective, however, the contract terms must be tailored to the individual business transaction, and they must reflect the needs and concerns of the individual parties. Just as you should not attempt to perform a medical procedure requiring specialized veterinary knowledge, you also should not try to draft a complicated contract without specialized legal knowledge.

Sources for generic contracts and other written agreements are included in the Resources section of this book. The authors do not endorse the use of fill-in-the-blank contracts; the information is provided as a guide only, with the recommendation that you consult an attorney to help adapt the generic agreements for your individual needs.

CHAPTER 3

Sales and Leases

Sales, and to a much lesser extent leases, are the lifeblood of the horse business. Breeding, showing, racing — all are driven by the prospect of a sale, and when the Greens decided to purchase a competition/broodmare prospect, their long-range goal was to sell the mare's produce after her retirement from the arena. Because the popularity of dressage is growing where the Greens live, and because their children are interested in competing in that discipline, the Greens decide on a warmblood. Because they cannot afford a proven competitor, they opt for a three-year-old filly offered for sale privately by a breeder in another state.

The filly is relatively well-bred, and the Greens like her looks when they visit her breeder and owner. The price, a little higher than they expected to spend, still is manageable, and the Greens and the breeder tentatively agree on the sale. Because the Greens discussed their potential purchase with their attorney *before* visiting the breeder and falling in love with the filly, they insisted on a written sales agreement. Because the transaction is for cash, the agreement can be relatively straightforward. (An installment purchase is more complicated, and will be discussed later in this chapter.)

The sales agreement should include, at a minimum:

• Name and full address of both the buyer and seller.

• Name and description of the horse, including any identifying tattoos or brands.

• Statement that the horse is registered (with registration number), or is eligible for registration, if applicable.

• The selling price.

• Sales tax responsibility. (The seller generally is responsible for collecting a state's sales tax, if the tax is applicable to the sale of horses. Whether the tax is collected from the buyer does not affect the seller's liability for the tax, and a careful seller will make certain that the buyer understands that he or she must add the tax to the purchase price.)

• A description of the general health and soundness of the horse.

• A statement attesting to soundness and suitability for a particular purpose, such as racing, competition, or breeding, if applicable.

• The place, date, and circumstances of transfer from seller to buyer, and which party will bear the risk of loss until the transfer. The agreement also should indicate which party will be responsible for board, veterinary, and farrier charges prior to the transfer. The contract also should include the sale or lease date and the signatures of all parties to the contract.

• A statement attesting that the seller is the owner of the horse and has the right to sell the animal, along with the disclosure of any existing liens.

• A clause identifying which jurisdiction's laws will govern disputes arising from the transaction. This may not be important when the seller and buyer live in the same state; it becomes more important for interstate and international sales.

• Any other warranties or disclaimers by the seller.

The last item can be particularly important if the seller attempts to disclaim all warranties. Most of us are familiar with the idea of buying a second-hand car or used appliance "as is," but we may not be aware that a horse can be sold under the same terms. When a seller insists on disclaiming all warranties on a horse, selling the animal "as is," the effect is that the buyer accepts the animal with no guarantees at all.

An "as is" sale should alert a prudent buyer to the possibility that the animal has a serious problem. A private seller has an ethical obligation, and possibly a legal one as well, to disclose any known disease, injury, or congenital defect to a buyer who asks specific questions, but "buyer beware" is good advice in any transaction.

The sales agreement also should include language making the sale contingent on a satisfactory pre-sale examination of the horse by a veterinarian. It is important to understand what such an examination can, and cannot, accomplish. The American Association of Equine Practitioners (AAEP) has issued "Guidelines for Reporting Purchase Examinations," which outline the requirements of a pre-purchase veterinary examination.

In brief, the examining veterinarian should give you a report in writing identifying the horse and indicating the date and place of the examination. The report should include "all abnormal or undesirable findings," and the veterinarian should "give his or her qualified opinion as to the functional effect of these findings." The veterinarian should not state an opinion about the suitability of the horse to a particular purpose, however, and you should not demand one.

The position of the AAEP is that suitability for a particular purpose is a business decision that should be made by the buyer, based on a variety of factors, only one of which is the purchase examination. If you are new to the horse business, you should consider having your trainer, or some other more experienced person, accompany you to examine the horse.

A final consideration for the Greens is whether to insure their new horse. If they choose to do so, advance arrangements should be made with the insurance carrier so that the horse can be covered from the time the sale is finalized.

BUYING ON TIME

The Greens purchased their new filly with cash, and they received a bill of sale as a receipt. Another option, especially for expensive animals, is an installment purchase, similar to buying an automobile and financing it for a number of months. Sometimes bank financing is used, particularly in parts of the country where the horse business represents an important part of the economy, but more often the seller agrees to accept installment payments for the horse. Whether you are an installment seller or an installment buyer, you should take all possible steps to protect yourself. The process is complex and fraught with danger for the unwary seller or buyer. The advice of an attorney is highly recommended, either to draft the sales agreement or to review an agreement you are asked to sign.

Most important — and this should not come as a surprise — is that the installment purchase agreement should be in writing. In addition to the elements of a cash sales agreement, an installment agreement should address, at a minimum, the following:

• The fact that the seller retains a security interest in the horse until the purchase price is paid in full. Security interests are discussed more fully in other portions of this book. Basically, a security interest in a horse allows the seller to keep his or her hand, legally, on the animal until the price is paid in full. It also might be advisable for the seller to require the buyer to execute a promissory note for the purchase price. By doing so, the seller has additional protection if the buyer defaults.

• The payment terms, and any penalty due if the buyer is late making one or more payments. The agreement also should set out in detail the circumstances that will constitute default.

• A requirement that, until the purchase price is paid in full, the buyer provide adequate veterinary, care, farrier care, food, and shelter for the horse.

• A requirement that, until the purchase price is paid in full, the buyer will maintain adequate insurance on the horse. (Although desirable protection for the seller, requiring insurance may not be economically feasible for many buyers.)

• Authorization to recover attorney fees if one party defaults and legal action is necessary to enforce the contract.

PUBLIC OR PRIVATE?

From your local stockyard to the select summer yearling sales at Keeneland, buying and selling at public auction differs from a private sale in at least one important aspect: the presence of a third party. Unlike a private sale, where the parties deal directly with each other, both the buyer and seller at an auction deal directly with the auction company. The buyer and seller may have direct contact when a horse is shown to a potential buyer prior to the sale, for example, but the mechanics of the sale are handled by the sales company.

For those unfamiliar with horse auctions, the process works like this: After locating a suitable auction, the seller enters into a written contract with the sales company. Depending on the auction, the seller also may have to pay a consignment fee for the horse. The consignment contract likely will be a complicated document setting out the rights and responsibilities of the seller and the auction company. Among other things, the contract should cover how bidding disputes will be resolved, how the title will be transferred from seller to buyer, the risk of loss, payment terms, and choice of law.

The contract also should include warranties, or guarantees,

made by the seller to the sales company. Buyers then rely upon these warranties at the auction. Most disputes arising from sales of horses at public auctions relate, either directly or indirectly, to alleged breaches of these warranties. If you are the seller, you should disclose any problems your horse might have; if you are the buyer, you should inspect the horse both before and immediately after the sale. Delaying an inspection could affect your rights if there is a problem.

Generally, and this will vary from sales company to sales company (and sometimes between different auctions conducted by the same company), there will be no express or implied warranties as to fitness for a particular purpose, soundness, condition, or respiratory health, for horses in the auction, and the buyer must be aware of these limitations. Some conditions, such as vision defects and the fact that the horse is a cribber or wobbler, or has undergone invasive surgery, generally should be announced by the sale company, given that accurate information about those conditions has been provided by the seller.

After making a successful final bid on a horse, the buyer signs an "acknowledgment of purchase" form identifying the purchaser and indicating the sales price and other pertinent information. The agreement also provides that the buyer will be bound by the conditions of sale printed in the catalogue. After settling the bill with the auction company, the buyer is allowed to remove the animal from the grounds. The sales company then pays the purchase price, less a commission, to the seller.

An auction company's "Conditions of Sale" and "Acknowledgment of Purchase" are contracts that establish the rights and responsibilities of the sales company, the seller, and the buyer. Like any other contract, they should be scrutinized, preferably with the advice of your attorney, before signing.

Whether to buy or sell a horse privately or at public auction is both a personal and a business decision. The advantages of a public auction, such as a larger pool of potential

Acknowledgement of Purchase and Security Agreement

Date _____   Sale Date _____

Hip Number _____   Purchase Price _____

Please print the following information:

Purchaser or Agent Name _____

Address _____

_____

City, State, Zip Code, Country _____

Telephone _____

The purchaser hereby purchases and promises to pay the Keeneland Association the purchase price set forth for the horse described herein plus Kentucky sales tax at the rate of 6 % of the purchase price unless exempt under KRS 139.531 (2) (a) and (2) (b) (see below). **This purchase and payment therefore is made in accordance with the additional terms and conditions set forth on the back hereof and incorporated by reference herein.** In order to secure payment of the purchase price, the purchaser hereby grants Keeneland Association, its successors and assigns, a security interest in and to the above described horse, and any other horses purchased, and any proceeds, progeny, and/or products thereof.

Purchaser acknowledges that he is familiar with the "Conditions of Sale" as printed in the catalogue and **the confirmation of purchase is subject to those conditions, the same being made a part hereof and incorporated by reference herein.**

OTHER THAN THOSE LIMITED WARRANTIES EXPRESSLY STATED ┌ ONDITIONS OF SALE, THERE ARE NO WARRANTIES, EXPRESS OR IMPLIF┌ ┐ PARTY OR CONSIGNOR AS TO MERCHANTABILITY OR FITNESS FOR A┌ ┐SE OF ANY ANIMAL SOLD AND ALL ANIMALS ARE SOLD "AS IS".

Purchaser claims exemption fro~

1. _____ The purchase is made for breeding p~
2. _____ The purchase is made by a non-~ ~ (2) years of age and will
   immediately be transporte~ ~ng holding of the horse in
   Kentucky for trainin~
3. _____ The horse purch~ ~ediately shipped by Keeneland Association,
   Inc. as ager. ~ to the purchaser at an out-of-state point via
   licensed Inte. ~erstood and agreed that such shipment shall be wholly
   at purchaser's . ~ be issued to ICC carrier upon receipt of bill of lading.

Notice: The purchaser ~ ~ement with Keeneland for the full purchase price not later than thirty minutes from the fall ~ammer or have approved credit with Keeneland for this sale. The individual signing this agreement, regardless of the form of the signature or his signing capacity, agrees to be personally liable, jointly and severally with the purchaser, for the full purchase price if the purchaser does not make settlement within thirty minutes or have approved credit or if Keeneland has not been provided a signed buyer's authorized agent form granting purchase authority during this sale to the individual signing this agreement.

OFFICE COPY

Signature _____

Print Signature Name _____

Billing address if different than above _____

City, State, Zip Code, Country _____

Telephone _____

An example of a purchase agreement.

buyers, a professional atmosphere, and the fact that there is a middleman to help collect the purchase price, may be offset by the sales commission that reduces your profit, the feeling that your horse is a small fish in a big pond, and the potential for less direct contact with the buyers.

A NEW TWIST ON AN OLD PROBLEM

A recent development begun at some major Thoroughbred auctions is the "repository," a system which allows a consignor to provide radiographs, videotapes of endoscopic examinations, and certificates and other explanations of the radiographs and endoscopic exams from a veterinarian. The veterinary information is then made available to buyers.

The use of a repository of veterinary information is a response by sales companies to the growing reliance by buyers on pre-sale veterinary examinations of sale horses. Consignors were complaining that repeated radiographic and endoscopic examinations were adversely affecting their horses, and buyers were complaining about the cost of such exams. By maintaining a repository of pertinent veterinary information, sales companies hope to reduce the complaints of both sellers and buyers.

Repositories have gotten mixed reviews in the few years since their inception. From the buyer's perspective, the repository might reduce the need for a pre-purchase exam, but it will not reduce a buyer's need to be diligent. The fact that such a service is provided by a sales company creates a duty on the part of the buyer to use the information. A buyer probably will have difficulty asserting a legal claim based upon a defect in a horse that could have been detected through a review of repository records, if those records were not reviewed. Unless you have specialized veterinary knowledge, you probably will need to pay a veterinarian to interpret the medical information provided in the repository, which can add to the overall cost of buying the horse. It also can prevent an expensive mistake.

Conditions of Sale at Keeneland, located in Lexington, Kentucky, for example, include a requirement that buyers "fully inspect" any horse that they may purchase, and the Conditions make an examination of information in the repository a necessary part of the full inspection. In other words, if you intend to purchase a horse at an auction that provides a repository of veterinary information, you should include a review of the provided information as part of your examination of the horse. You also should be aware that provision of veterinary information in a repository may make it unnecessary for a sales company to announce certain physical conditions of a horse prior to sale.

A buyer also should keep in mind that the sales company generally will not guarantee the accuracy of the information provided in a horse's repository file. The sale company acts only as a place for the seller and buyer to exchange information, but not as a guarantor of the information.

Although a buyer must review material in a repository, participation in the program by a seller generally is voluntary. If you are selling horses at a sale where a repository is provided, you may not have to participate as a requirement for selling in the auction. You should make the necessary inquiries of the sales company to determine if there is a repository, and if you are required to participate.

If you do participate, you may spare your horse the aggravation of repeated veterinary examinations, but you also will be responsible for the cost of the veterinary services necessary to provide information to the repository. This can be a significant part of your profit margin, particularly if you are not expecting a high price for the horse being sold. You also may be unintentionally warranting the condition of your horse by including veterinary information in a repository. For a repository program to be successful, it is important that sellers provide accurate, up-to-date information, and it is important that buyers use the service.

LEASING, A VIABLE ALTERNATIVE?

Sometimes, for a variety of reasons, you may want the use of a horse without actually buying him. This is often the case when you want to compete with a horse for a show season or two, or when you want to raise a foal without owning the broodmare. A lease may be the answer.

Leasing a horse is a lot like renting an automobile. The owner allows you to use the horse for a specified purpose, for a specified period of time, and you agree to pay for that use. You also agree to accept responsibility for providing adequate food, shelter, and care during the time the horse is in your possession.

A proper lease agreement should identify the parties and the horse, the term of the lease, and the amount of money to be paid by the "lessee" to the "lessor." The lease also should set out in detail the schedule of lease payments, recourse of the horse owner if the lease payments are not made on time, and the fact that the owner can recover attorney's fees if the lease is broken by the lessee. The document should state the purpose of the lease (whether the horse will be shown, or bred, for example), and any warranty the owner wishes to make about the suitability of the horse to the stated purpose. Whenever possible, the owner should insist that the lessee provide insurance, either mortality, loss of use, or both, on the horse. This can be prohibitively expensive for many lessees, however.

Finally, many lease agreements include an option to purchase the horse. If you decide on this option, the terms of the future sale (date, price, whether the sale will be cash or installment) should be included.

Everyone in the horse business probably will buy, sell, or lease a horse. The familiarity of the transaction should not make you complacent, however, and you should be certain of your rights and insist on recognition of these rights in a written agreement.

CHAPTER 4

Security Interests and Liens

Unpaid bills can be the ruin of any business. Whether you operate a large training stable or a modest boarding farm, the way you deal with the inevitable client who cannot, or will not, pay the bills may determine whether your business succeeds or fails. Fortunately, the impact of unpaid bills can be minimized through a little advance planning.

There is an obvious solution to unpaid bills for many service providers — simply quit the job, cut your losses, and go home. This option generally is not available to the person who boards or trains horses for others, however. Unlike a barn painter, who can limit his loss by refusing to finish the job when the client refuses to pay, a person who boards horses assumes a moral (and often legal) responsibility for the welfare of the animals.

Horses neither know nor care whether their board bills are being paid. Blissfully unaware of their owners' financial problems, they continue to eat, occupy a stall or pasture, and require veterinary care and farrier services on a regular basis. A trainer may be able to suspend the conditioning of a client's horse until the bill is paid, but there are both legal and humane reasons to continue to provide for the basic needs of the horses boarding at your farm. The result is a delinquent board bill that continues to grow, while your

Forms of ownership include partnerships, which are fairly common in horse racing.

Owners must "materially participate" in running an equine business to be able to deduct losses.

Boarding contracts can protect both the owner and client; an important clause in a boarding contract deals with authorization for emergency veterinary care.

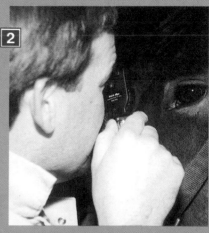

A sales agreement should include language making the sale contingent
upon a satisfactory pre-sale examination (photos 1 & 2); at many
public auctions, horses are basically sold "as is."

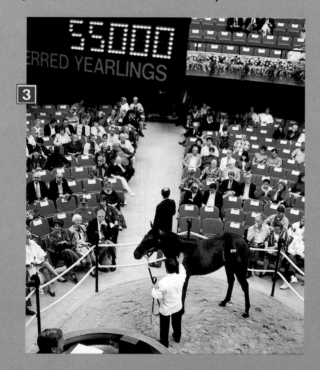

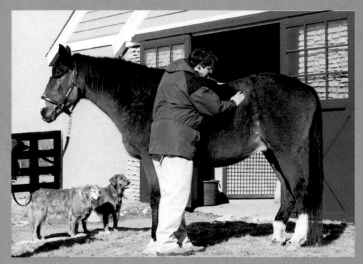

Kentucky is one state in which a statutory lien has been created in favor of a veterinarian for work done.

A security interest clause in a boarding agreement can give the owner of a boarding operation the right to sell a horse to satisfy a delinquent board bill.

Horses, by their very nature, can seem like accidents waiting to happen — not to mention accident prone. Numerous liability issues surround horse ownership or involvement. A "legal audit" of your horse business can identify potential problem areas and possible solutions.

Posting signs, such as those that warn of possibly dangerous
conditions, can help set the standard for non-negligent conduct.

WARNING
UNDER COLORADO LAW,
N EQUINE PROFESSIONAL IS NOT LIABLE
OR AN INJURY TO OR THE DEATH OF A
PARTICIPANT IN EQUINE ACTIVITIES
RESULTING FROM THE INHERENT RISKS
OF EQUINE ACTIVITIES, PURSUANT TO
SECTION 13-21-120,
COLORADO REVISED STATUTES.

A number of states have approved laws that limit the liability of farm and horse owners and sponsors of equine activities.

WARNING
Under Georgia law, an equine activity sponsor or equine professional is not liable for an injury to or the death resulting from the inherent risks of equine activities pursuant to Chapter 12 of Title 4 of the Official Code of Georgia Annotated.

WARNING
UNDER KENTUCKY LAW, A FARM
ANIMAL ACTIVITY SPONSOR, FARM
ANIMAL PROFESSIONAL, OR OTHER
PERSON DOES NOT HAVE THE DUTY TO
ELIMINATE ALL RISKS OF INJURY OF
PARTICIPATION IN FARM ANIMAL
ACTIVITIES. THERE ARE INHERENT
RISKS OF INJURY THAT YOU VOLUN-
TARILY ACCEPT IF YOU PARTICIPATE
IN FARM ANIMAL ACTIVITIES.

It makes sense to wear a safety helmet when involved in potentially dangerous activities like fox hunting and jumping.

profit margin shrinks.

The Greens do not depend on the income from their boarding enterprise for their livelihood, but they feel the effects of delinquent bills just like the owners of any other business. Fortunately, the "legal audit" conducted by their attorney produced some good advice and an important addition to the written boarding contract they use with their clients.

Their attorney's advice included a healthy dose of preventive medicine, aimed at keeping the problem of overdue bills from developing in the first place. First, screen your clients. This does not always mean a full-blown credit check, but when you are approached by a potential boarder that you do not know, you should ask for references. If you ask for references, take the next step and check them. If your potential boarder has kept his or her horse at several different farms in the last few months, that should be a red flag.

> ## AT A GLANCE
>
> - Ask for and check a potential boarder's references.
>
> - Identify delinquent bills as soon as possible.
>
> - Security interest clauses can aid boarding farms in recouping unpaid bills.
>
> - Be aware of your state's specific statutes regarding agister's liens.

Second, keep your record-keeping up to date and bill regularly. Many small business owners — farm owners included — are not very good at bookkeeping, but at the same time they cannot afford to hire an accountant. If you are in this position, bite the bullet, buy a small business bookkeeping software package and learn to use it.

Finally, identify delinquent bills as soon as possible and make the client aware that there is a problem. If your initial contact with the client is by telephone, follow up with a letter. If you are forced into court, a thorough paper trail often will help you recover an overdue bill. Clients occasionally forget to pay a bill, of course, and checks really can be lost in the mail. The sooner you inform a client about a payment problem, the sooner the problem can be resolved.

Sometimes, though, your best efforts are not good enough, and you find yourself with a growing stack of board bills that you know will not be paid. To deal with such a situation, the Greens' attorney recommended that they make some changes in their standard boarding contract.

The first addition to the Greens' boarding contract was a clause requiring payment in full within 10 days of the statement date, along with a provision allowing the Greens to charge interest (1.5% per month is fairly standard) on any outstanding balance not paid within 30 days. The Greens also added a clause allowing them to recover attorney fees if they have to go to court to recover a delinquent account.

The second addition to the Greens' contract was a clause granting them a security interest in the horses boarded at their farm. A simple security interest clause could include the following (or similar) language:

To secure full payment of all charges due under this boarding contract, including attorney fees, the owner of the horse, or horses, identified in Paragraph _____ hereby grants to Peter and Mary Green a security interest in said horses. In addition, the owner authorizes the Greens and their agents to act as attorney-in-fact for the owner for the purpose of executing any financial statements or other documents which the Greens, in their sole discretion, shall deem necessary to perfect the security interest granted herein. Upon failure of the owner of the horse, or horses, identified in Paragraph _____ to make payment in full within thirty (30) days following receipt of a statement, the Greens may declare the owner to be in default and they may exercise all rights granted to a secured party under the laws of the state of _____.

Depending on your state laws, the rights referred to may include the right to sell the horse, at public auction or privately, to recover the delinquent board bill. Such laws generally require that you give the horse owner notice of the pending sale. If you sell the horse for a sum greater than the delinquent board bill and the costs associated with the sale, that excess amount usually must be returned to the owner.

You also may have to file certain documents to make your security interest valid (a legal process called "perfecting" the lien). The best way to learn the intricacies of your state's laws regarding secured creditors is to consult your attorney. Do not relay solely on this book, or any other generic reference.

If you choose to include a security interest clause in your boarding contracts, you also should require that the horse owner identify any outstanding liens on the animal. Otherwise, you might wind up as one of several creditors claiming proceeds from the sale of the horse.

What if, unlike the Greens, you do not use written contracts, or your contract does not include a security interest clause? At this point, you may get some significant help from the laws of your state, if you know where to look. While specifics vary from jurisdiction to jurisdiction, statutes in many states provide for liens in favor of farms that board horses. Often termed "agister's liens" (an agister is a person in the business of boarding livestock for a fee as a bailee), they give the lienholder the right to retain or dispose of property for satisfaction of a debt. (Although this sounds a lot like the security interest discussed earlier, the requirements and effect can be significantly different.)

Even if "agister's lien" is an unfamiliar term, chances are good that you have had experience with liens before. If you borrowed money to buy a car or truck, for example, the lender probably retained an interest in the vehicle. That interest is a lien, and it protects the lender by creating the right to repossess the vehicle if you do not keep up the monthly payments. A lien also enables a lender to recover his money if the vehicle is sold before the loan is satisfied.

In theory, at least, an agister's lien statute gives a farm owner the right to sell a client's horse and use the proceeds to satisfy the delinquent board bill. In practice, however, things usually are not that simple. Terminology of agister's lien statutes varies from state to state, and it is essential that a farm owner be aware of the nuances of his or her state's law before taking any action involving a client's horse.

In some states, for example, a person who boards horses on a farm that is leased rather than owned may not be a qualified lienholder. In such a circumstance, an attempt to sell a client's horse to cover a board bill could be conversion, a legal term for taking another person's property without the right to do so. There can be civil penalties, and possibly criminal charges in some states, levied against the seller.

There are many other questions that must be answered based on your state's specific statutes. This chapter provides some general direction, but for answers directly related to the circumstances at your boarding farm, you should consult an attorney familiar with your state laws and with equine issues.

• When does the lien take effect?

In some states, the lien comes into existence at the time the board charges are incurred, without any further action on the farm owner's part. Some other states' statutes require a farm owner to take subsequent action, often in court, to validate the lien. The distinction is important. If the statute requires some action by the farm owner to perfect the lien, such as posting public notices prior to the sale of the client's horse or filing an action in court, the farm owner has no right to sell or retain the client's horse until the required action is taken. In a state where a farm owner must perfect the lien in some manner, prior sale of the horse could amount to conversion, and the farm owner could wind up with legal bills far in excess of the delinquent board bill.

• What happens if the horse is returned to the owner before the board bill is paid?

In some states, the farm owner has a lien on a client's horse only so long as the horse remains in the possession of the lienholder. In those states, your lien will be defeated if you return the horse to the client while the bill is still outstanding. The circumstances under which the client regains possession also may be important. A client who slips onto the farm under cover of night to take back his or her horse may not defeat the lien, and he or she may be guilty of trespassing as well.

In other states, validity of the lien does not depend on whether the farm owner has retained the horse or returned the animal to the client. In those states where the lien is not defeated by return of the horse to the client, the farm owner retains a secured interest in the horse even after the animal is returned to the client and the lienholder should be able to demand satisfaction of the lien if the horse later is sold.

• What are the consequences if the farm owner refuses to return the horse to the client upon demand?

Because of the potential problems that can arise if the horse is returned to the client, generally it is to the farm owner's advantage to retain possession of the horse if possible. Some states' statutes give the farm owner the explicit right to retain the horse, while other statutes do so only implicitly. If a farm owner has no right to retain the horse, refusal to return the animal to the owner upon demand could amount to conversion and might result in civil and/or criminal penalties.

• If your state's statutes authorize sale of the horse to satisfy the lien, how must the sale be conducted?

State statutes also differ in the requirements they impose for a valid sale to satisfy an agister's lien, and a farm owner must be familiar with the requirements of his or her locale. There may be, for example, time limits imposed by law that a farm owner must observe. A few statutes allow the lien holder to conduct the sale of the horse himself or herself if there is proper notice, but in almost all cases it is safer for the farm owner to enter the horse in a recognized sale, if possible. Satisfying a lien by selling the horse at a recognized auction may generate a higher price, and also will make it more difficult for the client to claim later that the horse was not sold for a fair price.

• If a horse must be sold to satisfy a lien, how are the proceeds of the sale distributed?

There will be many situations when the farm owner is not the only party with a security interest. A bank that has loaned money to a person to buy a horse probably has a secured interest in the animal (just as the bank retained a lien on your car), and there also may be other statutory liens. You may need an attorney's help if there are competing interests.

In Kentucky, for example, a statutory lien also is created in favor of a veterinarian for work done, and the priority of competing interests must be resolved before sale proceeds can be distributed. In other words, even if you do everything required under your state's statutes, you still might be unable to recover the full amount of the overdue bills. There also will be situations in which the attorney fees and other costs associated with recovering an overdue bill are larger than the bill itself. You need to be prepared to cut your losses and give up if necessary. In sum, agister's lien statutes create significant rights for a farm owner, but those statutes can be minefields for the unwary. The statutory requirements must be followed or your rights may not be protected. And some agister's lien statutes may allow you to recover only board charges, but not third-party charges such as payments you make to a farrier, veterinarian, or van service. It is better to know the fine points of your state's statutory lien scheme before you need to put the law into effect.

Some statutes also might be unconstitutional because they do not provide for sufficient due process notice and hearing requirements. If courts in your state have questioned the constitutionality of local agister's lien statutes, and possibly found them lacking, it might be safer to sue in state court for the delinquent board bill, then proceed as a judgment creditor. You need an attorney's advice here. Judicial determination of a lien's validity will help forestall subsequent questions from the delinquent client. Depending on the bill's size, you may be able to proceed in small claims court without an attorney.

In the best of all possible worlds, all your clients would pay their bills on time. No one lives in that world, of course, and the inevitability of unpaid board bills should encourage you to include a security interest clause in your written boarding contracts. This will facilitate the process if you are forced to sell a boarder's horse to satisfy a delinquent bill.

LEARN TO COMMUNICATE

What if the shoe is on the other foot, and you find yourself unable to pay a board or training bill? What should you do? What are your options?

In such a situation, contact the farm owner or trainer immediately and explain the problem. Most people will try and work with a client who is making an honest attempt to pay his or her bills; the sooner you can start the process, the better for everyone. A farm owner who knows you are having trouble paying a bill, but that you also are trying to solve the problem, will be less likely to resort to collection measures. Good communication between you and the farm owner or trainer is never more important than when there is a dispute over a bill.

Agister's lien statutes are written to protect a farm owner who has provided a service and incurred expenses boarding a horse for a client, when the client does not pay. The deck, therefore, is stacked somewhat in favor of the lien holder. The delinquent client does have some rights, though. If a creditor attempts to retain your horse, or to sell the animal to satisfy a board bill, for example, you should contact an attorney immediately to determine what your rights are under the particular circumstances. In addition to those discussed here, you might have rights under the Fair Debt Practices Act.

If there is a written agreement between you and the farm owner or trainer, that agreement should spell out the circumstances under which the creditor can declare you in default, and the measures that he or she can take to recover the debt. If the contract requirements are not followed, you may have a legal cause of action against the farm owner.

The best way to avoid problems is to pay your bills on time, but sometimes that is impossible. If you cannot pay, inform the other party, explain why, and set out your plan to deal with the problem.

CHAPTER 5

Liability Issues

The popularity of Judge Wapner's "Animal Court," Judge Koch's "The People's Court," "Judge Judy," "Judge Mills Lane," "Judge Joe Brown," and other similar "legal reality" television shows convinced the Greens that everyone wants to sue everyone else, with national exposure, if possible. They recognize that their modest horse business is a potential minefield of liability, but they are not sure how to either evaluate or minimize the risks.

Horses often seem to be accidents waiting to happen, and most owners can recount at least one horror story that starts with: "You aren't going to believe this, but…" Less apparent, but equally true, is the realization that horse businesses, by their very nature, can be "accident prone." Whether horses are your vocation or avocation, it is important to shield yourself from as much potential liability as possible. Failure to do so can be devastating, both personally and professionally.

Liability is an extremely broad legal concept, encompassing everything from an obligation to repay a debt to the responsibility a person has for the consequences of his or her actions. For someone in the horse business, liability lurks behind every stall door, in every paddock, on every trail, and in every business transaction. When you buy a load of hay on credit, for example, you are incurring a liability, in this case the obligation to pay for the hay at some point in the future. Such liability, voluntarily assumed, is part of the normal course of doing business, and is not the type of liability that concerns the Greens.

More troublesome is the potential liability that results when your actions cause harm to a third party. The sources are endless. If you board horses for other owners, you might be responsible for damages if one of those horses becomes injured

AT A GLANCE

- Identify potential problem areas and plan accordingly.

- Include an attorney, accountant, and insurance agent on your business team.

- Contracts should include a waiver of liability.

while in your care. If you give riding lessons, you might be liable for injuries suffered by one of your riders. If you open your land for trail rides, you might be liable if a horse or rider gets hurt on your property. If you sell a horse, you may have a duty to disclose certain physical conditions of the animal, and you might be liable for damages if you do not do so. If a horse escapes from your property and causes injury to a person, another animal, or someone's property, you might find yourself responsible.

If you lease your horse to another person, you might be liable if the horse injures the lessee. If an employee becomes injured, you might be liable. If you agree to transport another person's horse in your trailer, you might be liable if the horse in injured. You may even incur liability by doing nothing more than keeping your own horses on your own property. This could happen if a court finds that the horses are an "attractive nuisance," and thus an unreasonable danger to trespassing children who are injured. The list continues.

Adequate insurance helps, and you should discuss your needs with a reputable insurance agent who is familiar with the horse business. It should be obvious, though, that the only way to truly insulate yourself from all potential liability is to abandon the horse business altogether. Few of us are willing to do that, however, and the next best thing is to identify potential problem areas and plan accordingly. Accidents do happen, no matter how careful you are, and there is always a risk that you will find yourself on the wrong end of a lawsuit. Being blameless does not make you immune from a lawsuit, and being right does not guarantee that you will win in court if you are sued. Even if you do win, you likely will be faced with thousands of dollars in legal bills. When dealing with potential liability, it is always better to be safe than sorry.

The Greens decide on a preemptive strike, a visit to their attorney before any problems arise. With their attorney they can review plans for their horse operation, and the attorney can suggest ways to minimize the risk. Attorneys like having a client ask them, ahead of time: "This is what I plan to do. Are there problems?" Attorneys hate having a client tell them, after the fact: "This is what I did. Can you fix it?"

PRACTICE PREVENTIVE LEGAL MEDICINE

Many attorneys endorse the concept of a "legal audit," a review of your horse business with emphasis on potential problem areas and possible solutions. If you board horses and do not require written contracts with your boarders, for example, your attorney can recognize the need and draft a suitable document. If you do use a written contract, your attorney can suggest changes, if needed. After reviewing your plans and aspirations, your attorney can identify, and thus help you avoid, many of the pitfalls on the path to your business goals.

Whatever your objectives in the horse business — from owning a safe and sound pleasure horse, to managing a band of productive broodmares, to competing successfully on the "A" show circuit — you probably already rely on the expertise of a team of professionals. A veterinarian and farrier are essential members of the team, no matter what the activity, and depending on your goals you may also need a trainer for your horse and a coach to help hone your own riding skills.

Just as important is your business team. The members

should be selected with care, and should include an accountant, an attorney, and an insurance agent. All should be familiar with the horse industry. A good accountant can be the difference between a business that shows a profit and one that does not, by offering financial planning and bookkeeping services and by guiding you through the maze of state and federal tax laws and workers' compensation requirements. Your attorney and insurance agent can help guard your investment, the former by anticipating problems and drafting written agreements to protect your interests and the latter by providing adequate insurance coverage. An attorney also can help you operate your business in compliance with local or state laws, among the most important of which are those designed to limit your liability in certain situations.

Locating professionals with experience in the horse business can be simple or difficult, depending on where you live. Personal referrals from other horse owners in your area are probably the best recommendations, and some states' bar associations offer lawyer referral services for attorneys. It is important that the team understands how your business operates now, and your goals for the future. You should have the team in place before you need their services. Prevention and risk management, not damage control, should be your goals.

Some of the issues raised by the Greens with their attorney include how to operate their business, a review of the contracts they use, the necessity of acting reasonably to minimize potential liability, and the effect of state law on their liability.

SO WHAT'S ATTRACTIVE ABOUT A NUISANCE?

A field of horses is a magnet for children, tempting some of them to climb a fence to play with the animals. If a child trespasses on your property and is injured by one of your horses, are you liable for the child's injuries? Trespassers generally are accorded little protection, but an exception is made for trespassing children if they fall under the umbrella of the "attractive nuisance" doctrine.

A land owner generally is liable for injuries to trespassing children if: (1) the farm owner knows, or has reason to know, that children trespass on his or her property; (2) the farm owner knows, or has reason to know, that there is a condition on the property (in this case, grazing horses) that poses an unreasonable risk of harm to such children; (3) the children, because of their youth, are not likely to recognize the danger posed by the horses; (4) the farm owner does not exercise reasonable care to protect the children; and, (5) correcting the condition is relatively easy. If horses in a field are an attractive nuisance, you may be liable for injuries incurred by trespassing children.

Laws on attractive nuisance vary from state to state, and you should consult an attorney for help interpreting the law and court decisions in your particular jurisdiction. In Kentucky, for example, horses in a field generally are not considered an attractive nuisance, possibly because of the importance of the horse industry to the state's economy. Your situation may be different, however, and it may be necessary to take particular measures to protect trespassing children. This is another situation where a "legal audit" of your business may reap substantial benefits by identifying a potential problem before it becomes a real problem.

HOW DO I OWN THEE; LET ME COUNT THE WAYS

If you already have an established horse business, then you have made the decision about form of ownership in the past, possibly with little thought to the available options or to the potential ramifications of your choice. If so, now might be a good time to review that choice. If you are contemplating starting a business, on the other hand, selecting the proper form of ownership should be the first decision you make. In either case, you should rely on your team of professionals to explain the possibilities and their application to your unique situation.

A comprehensive discussion of the various forms of ownership appeared earlier in Chapter 1. In summary, a horse business can be operated as a sole proprietorship, partnership, or corporation. State law may give you other options as well, such as a limited liability company or partnership.

There is no correct choice for all situations, and the best option for your business depends on many factors. These factors include the level of individual control you intend to exercise over the operation, whether you need to raise operating capital, the relative tax benefit of each option, and how much personal responsibility for the debts and liabilities of the business you are willing to accept.

The choice you make now also may affect your future personal liability in case of a lawsuit against you and your business. Choosing to incorporate, for example, may prevent a successful litigant from reaching your personal assets. However, you should weigh that potential advantage against the increased administrative responsibilities and tax treatment another type of ownership plan might require before making a final decision.

GET IT IN WRITING

You have heard this before, but it merits repeating.

The horse business traditionally has operated on a handshake and a promise. This approach worked, more or less, for years, and many people still conduct their businesses this way. The old axiom that an oral contract is worth only the paper it is written on applies to any horse activity, making it prudent to obtain a written agreement for every significant business transaction. If you board horses, for example, have each horse owner sign a boarding contract that explains the responsibilities of the parties. If you give lessons, have your students (or their parents) sign contracts. If you offer trail riding, or make your land available for trail riding, have the participants sign a release. If you think this is too much trouble, think again.

Contracts should include an exculpatory clause, or waiver of liability, that excuses the party performing the service, the owner of a boarding farm, for example, from liability in the performance of the contract. The effect of such a clause is to limit the farm owner's liability in the event that the boarding horse or its owner is injured. You generally cannot protect yourself from negligent actions, no matter how well written the contract, which emphasizes the need to act reasonably at all times.

Whether such a waiver of liability can be enforced to prevent a lawsuit against the farm owner will depend on the laws of your particular state, and to a large extent on how well the clause is drafted. Even if there is no clear authority in your state for the enforceability of an exculpatory clause, and this varies from state to state, it is better practice to include such a waiver of liability in your boarding contracts. Some liability insurance policies require such language in a boarding contract, and a horse owner might be less likely to initiate a lawsuit if he or she has signed a waiver.

The value of a written contract depends entirely on how well the document is drafted, and you should consult your attorney for guidance. It is tempting to buy one of several available books of fill-in-the-blank legal forms, and run off a few copies at the local print shop. While this might make economic sense in the short run, it will be pure happenstance if one of those fill-in-the-blank contracts matches all — or any — of the requirements of your particular situation. One-size-fits-all legal forms can be a good starting point, but you and your attorney should review the document carefully and adapt it to your needs. It will be money well spent if a problem arises.

ACT REASONABLY

Probably the most important thing you can do to forestall a lawsuit is to conduct your business in a "reasonable" manner. The most frequent basis for liability is a claim that you acted negligently when someone is injured or when property is damaged. Generally, you can avoid being legally negligent simply by acting reasonably under the circumstances, but you must know what this standard of reasonable care means in practice.

Separating the paddocks of two aggressive breeding stallions with a double row of four-board plank fencing probably is reasonable conduct; separating those two stallions with a single strand of barbed wire probably is not. It is not sufficient that you did the best you could under the circumstances — perhaps a single strand of barbed wire is all you could afford — the standard of care is that of a hypothetical "reasonable person," not a specific individual. Nor is it always safe to do things the same as everyone else in your area. It is possible, although not likely, that everyone you know fails to meet the reasonable care standard.

On the other hand, reasonable care does not require a super-human effort. Nor does it require you to always adopt the best option. The fencing examples above represent two extremes, and there may be a middle ground that also would constitute reasonable care under the circumstances. Usually, reasonable care will be simple common sense: Make certain that your fences are in good repair and that there are no dangerous holes in the paddocks; inspect stall interiors for nails or other protruding objects; be aware of the physical condition of the horses in your care; hire competent help; and pay attention.

TAKE ADVANTAGE OF STATE LAW

An old joke asks: "What are the nine most frightening words in the English language?" The answer: "I'm from the government, and I'm here to help."

Negative perceptions aside, the government sometimes manages to do something that actually makes a horse business easier and more economical to run. One of the best examples in recent years is the passage, in most states, of laws that limit the liability of farm owners, horse owners, and sponsors of equine activities. As of this writing (Summer 1999), 43 states have some type of equine liability law on their books. Texts of the laws in your particular state can be found in statute books at college or local libraries, from your local legislators, on the Internet, or from an attorney. The last-named is the best source for advice on these laws.

Because the equine liability laws vary from state to state, a comprehensive, jurisdiction-specific discussion is beyond the scope of this book. Generally, though, the laws recognize that any equine activity has certain built-in risks, and that a farm owner or activity sponsor has a responsibility to warn participants of those risks. The laws generally do not impose on the owner or sponsor a duty to eliminate those inherent risks. In other words, the equine liability laws require participants in an equine activity to assume many of the risks associated with that activity.

Kentucky's equine liability law, found at Kentucky Revised Statutes 247.401-247.4029, is similar to laws in other states, and is illustrative of what these laws can and cannot do for a farm owner. Keep in mind, though, that the law in Kentucky is not the law in any other state, and you should get professional advice in interpreting and implementing the equine liability law in your jurisdiction. By the same token, you should not rely on the cursory treatment in this book as your only authority on Kentucky liability law. Your best guide is an attorney familiar with the topic.

Kentucky's equine liability law is applicable to most, but not all, equine activities. Horse shows and other competitions, training, boarding, trail rides, farrier and veterinary services are covered by the law. Most horse racing activities, questions arising from fencing problems, and liability of landowners to trespassers are not covered. The inherent risks of working with horses, such as the simple fact they are big, powerful animals that can hurt you, their general unpredictability, and the fact that other participants might act negligently, are covered. Negligent acts by the equine professional or sponsor, such as providing faulty tack or a dangerous horse, or the failure to post warning signs regarding known dangerous conditions on the land, are not covered. While the law does not protect a farm owner against his or her own negligence, it does set the standard for non-negligent conduct as "adherence…to the standards of care within the profession." In other words, you are not negligent if you act like a reasonable horse person would in similar circumstances.

Equine liability laws are "get out of jail free" cards for farm owners and other equine professionals in Kentucky, provided they are not negligent and they follow the statute's guidelines regarding proper notice to participants. To receive the benefits of the Kentucky law, a farm owner or other equine activity sponsor must post a warning notice, or notices, in a conspicuous place. The sign must contain the following language:

WARNING

Under Kentucky law, a farm activity sponsor, farm animal professional, or other person does not have the duty to eliminate all risks of injury of participation in farm animal activities. There are inherent risks of injury that you voluntarily accept if you participate in farm animal activities.

A similar notice must be included in all written contracts for professional equine services, including instruction and the rental of horses and/or tack for trail riding and other activities. If such a notice is not part of the contract, the farm owner will not be able to rely on the favorable (to him or her) statutory provisions in the event of a lawsuit. The chapter on contracts addressed the advisability of exculpatory clauses in contracts. Enforcement of an exculpatory clause that does not include any specific language required by statute is problematic.

Consultation with an attorney familiar with equine law can tell you whether your state has an equine liability law (the odds are good that it does), how the law operates, and what the law requires that you do. You should consider equine liability laws as sound advice about how to stay out of trouble. You ignore that advice at your own peril.

CHAPTER 6

Planning for the Future

The Greens' have recently acknowledged their mortality. Over the past 12 years, the Greens' horse boarding and trail riding business has been successful. They want to plan now to minimize estate and inheritance taxes. They want to provide for the continuation of the business, which they would like to leave to their children. Amy seems more interested than John in working in the family equine business.

Some of the discussion in this chapter will apply to everyone, not just owners of horses or horse businesses. We all need to consider some basic things, so they are included here, along with issues that apply specifically to horse business owners.

CAN SOMEONE ACT FOR YOU IF YOU BECOME ILL OR INJURED OR IF YOU ARE AWAY?

The Greens have told us they know they will die some day. That's a good start, as sometimes people find it difficult to discuss such matters. Many people are familiar with the concepts of health care surrogates and living wills, which tell family, medical personnel, and friends what medical choices you want made in the event of a terminal illness where you cannot inform the appropriate individuals at the time a decision needs to be made.

But the Greens also need to be sure that someone has authority to act for them if they cannot act for themselves in running their business. In part, this will depend on how their horse business is organized and run. It is important, however, that some person have the authority to order feed, write checks to pay bills, etc. Under many circumstances, but not all, a spouse can act on behalf of the other spouse. But what if the situation is one where that would not be possible?

> ## AT A GLANCE
>
> • Giving someone power of attorney is the simplest way for that person to act for you legally.
>
> • A letter of last instructions can arrange for your horses' care immediately following your death.
>
> • Trusts can be used to set up future care of your horses.
>
> • Leaving your horses to someone in your will may be the simplest option.

Often the simplest way to give someone legal permission to act for you is to appoint someone as attorney-in-fact, to act on your behalf. This is frequently called giving someone power of attorney. There are several ways to do this, and as you will see, you should make sure you know what kind of power of attorney you have and you should choose the person to act for you very carefully.

POWER OF ATTORNEY (OR GENERAL POWER OF ATTORNEY)

This form is available in all states and generally allows another person to do everything for you that you could have done for yourself. It does not take any power away from you to act in your own behalf. It takes immediate effect. When someone acts as attorney-in-fact for someone else, he or she usually must inform other parties that he or she is acting for someone else, by signing, for example, as "Martin Page, attorney-in-fact for Mary Green" or "Martin Page, POA for Mary Green." The general power of attorney does not extend into periods of your disability, however. This means that if the Greens, for example, choose to have this form of power of attorney, it requires that someone get court permission to act for them if they both become disabled.

DURABLE POWER OF ATTORNEY

This form of power of attorney is identical to the general power of attorney, except that it continues through periods of disability. It will contain a clause specifically giving authority to act during periods of disability. It also may include a description of the evidence necessary to establish disability in the grantor of the power. This is probably not necessary with this form of power of attorney as the attorney-in-fact has power to act now.

SPRINGING POWER OF ATTORNEY

This form comes into effect only when the grantor becomes disabled. It must specify the method in which disability is to be determined. Many people like this because they worry about the other forms giving the attorney-in-fact power too soon. This form is not recognized in all states, however, because statutes may not provide for it and courts can be more reluctant to accept that you really would have made this same choice at some nebulous point in the future. It seems easier for courts to accept the notion, as with the durable power of attorney, that a person you trust to act for you now also would be someone you would trust to act for you in periods of disability.

LIMITED OR SPECIAL PURPOSE POWER OF ATTORNEY

Unlike the other powers of attorney, this gives another person power to act on your behalf only in specific circumstances, or for a specific period of time. This avoids giving someone too much power, or giving it too soon, but it also requires a new document for any act not within the scope, or outside of the time limits, of the first document.

YOUR HORSES COULD STARVE BEFORE YOUR WILL IS PROBATED

It takes time to have a funeral, locate a will, get to court to have the will probated, and have the court appoint the executor. In the meantime, the horses need food and clean stalls, at the very least. Plan now to have them cared for immediately after death.

LETTER OF LAST INSTRUCTIONS

Peter and Mary are concerned about caring for the horses, and want to provide for them as well as they can after death. One of the things that worries them is immediate post-death care of both the boarded horses and their personal horses. The power of attorney no longer has effect once the grantor of the power dies. (While it might be tempting to assume that only one spouse will die leaving the other to handle the details, all too often spouses die together, or the health of the surviving spouse is too poor for that person to be able to deal with immediate personal or business details.) Obviously, if their business is such that they have other people around to provide short-term care, this may not be a problem. It frequently is a problem, however, especially for very small business operations and for horse owners who are not in business at all, but have horses. There are some things the Greens can do to deal with the problem of caring for the horses.

One of the best is for them each to prepare a letter of last instructions. This will handle the period between death and the time a will is probated. In addition to providing information about any funeral arrangements they may have made, or their wishes about funeral service, the document should name someone as interim caretaker for the horses. It should contain enough information to allow those acting on the basis of the letter to determine how to contact the owners of boarded horses. Depending on the circumstances, it also may be necessary for the letter to give permission for someone to enter onto the Greens' land to care for the horses.

In addition, the Greens should place the letter of last instructions in a place that can be reached quickly after their deaths. They could provide copies to key individuals soon after writing the letter. But they may not want to do that, for fear of confusing or complicating matters if, for example, they change their minds about something and decide to write a new letter of last instructions. So what else could they do?

The Greens could put the letter of last instructions in a safe, fireproof place. In some communities, ambulance and other emergency personnel are trained to look in the freezer for medical information about elderly persons. Nearly everyone has a refrigerator, it is usually easy to find, and is unlikely to be destroyed in a fire. This would be an ideal place for such a letter, if double wrapped in a sealable freezer bag. The Greens also can tell important people to look there for such documents. The freezer is probably preferable to a safe deposit box, at least in states where such boxes get sealed until the relevant representative of the state taxing authority can attend the first post-death opening.

PROVIDING FOR HORSES' CARE IMMEDIATELY AFTER DEATH

It will not be enough for the Greens to identify people to care for the horses immediately after their deaths. Any agreements or contracts with owners of boarded horses should explicitly specify not only the amount of payment, the services provided, etc., but should also specify whether the contract terminates in the event of the sudden death of the business owner(s), and how the transition will be handled. Someone may need immediate access to this information, so the Greens must make sure that the right people know where to find this information.

IS A TRUST THE THING?

Maybe you, like the Greens, have heard lots of stories, or maybe you've even read books about trusts. If so, you might wonder if a trust is the best thing for you to do to plan for the future. The following may help you decide.

REVOCABLE TRUSTS

Revocable trusts are also known as "living" trusts. Such

trusts take effect during the lifetime of the maker of the trust. They can be modified or completely revoked during the lifetime of the maker of the trust. This flexibility makes them ideal for certain circumstances.

In this case, the Greens may want to use a revocable trust for any horses they own. If they have a revocable trust, they can place ownership of the horses, and funds for the care of the horses, in the trust. They will have to name a trustee, but Mary or Peter, or both, can serve as trustee. The trust will take effect immediately and will not go through the probate process at their deaths. It might be a good idea to name John or Amy as successor trustee, in case Mary and Peter die together. Someone would then have the immediate ability to do whatever is necessary to care for the horses. This trust is ideally suited to provide a means for continued operation of a family farm or business. The trust is a separate legal entity and will file its own income tax returns through the trustee, who acts as fiduciary.

The Greens could, for example, place their own horses and funds, perhaps even a life insurance policy, in trust now. Even if a life insurance policy is included in the trust, some ready cash also will be necessary to care for the horses during the time between death and receipt of the proceeds of the policy.

Acting as their own trustees, the Greens can retain the right to sell the horses, or acquire others in trust, during their lifetimes if they so choose. The trust can be written so that either can act alone as trustee, or as survivor trustee should only one of them die. Because the trust is revocable, they can change their minds at any time. The Greens' trust, if they decide to take this option, should specify how and when the trust is to terminate. If the trust still exists at their deaths, the property in the trust will go to the named beneficiary or beneficiaries. The Greens really need to make sure they have a letter of last instructions because it can take some time to transfer legal ownership of the horses and other trust property, even though the living trust avoids the probate process.

Although the revocable trust can provide for the care of their horses without the delay of the probate process, such a trust will not reduce the size of their taxable estates, for estate tax purposes. The Internal Revenue Code contains several sections pertinent to trusts. Only those trusts over which the trust maker holds no strings will reduce the size of one's federal taxable estate. Because a revocable trust leaves the maker of the trust with the power to alter the terms of the trust or to revoke the trust entirely, such a trust would remain part of a decedent's (deceased's) federal taxable estate. The Greens will need to check with their legal and financial advisers to find out how their state treats revocable trusts.

IRREVOCABLE TRUSTS

During their lifetimes, the Greens also can establish an irrevocable trust. Like a revocable trust, an irrevocable trust avoids the delay of probate. If, however, the Greens decide to create an irrevocable trust, they will not, as makers of the trust, be able to remove ownership of a horse from the trust. They will not be able to remove funds from the trust, unless they appoint themselves as trustees. They can serve in that capacity, just as they could with a revocable trust. As trustees, they can exercise all the powers given to them under the terms of the trust. These terms may include, among other things, selling a horse. But remember those strings in the Internal Revenue Code?

If the Greens act as their own trustees, even though the trust is irrevocable, they will be said to have retained power for themselves, and the value of the property held by the trust will be included in the Greens' federal taxable estate(s). Even in the case of an irrevocable trust, they may decide to appoint John and/or Amy as trustee(s), if reducing the size of their taxable estates is more important than the flexibility of acting for themselves.

YOU COULD JUST LEAVE THE BUSINESS, HORSES INCLUDED, TO SOMEONE IN YOUR WILL

Mrs. Green heard a news report recently about a woman who left a million dollars in trust to her pet groundhog. She and Mr. Green want to know if they can provide for their horses through their wills. The short answer is maybe, but they need to remember that a will has to go through the probate process, making it even more imperative that they provide for the short term care of the horses.

HONORARY TRUSTS IN YOUR WILL

In some states, courts may not require or allow the executor of an estate to honor testamentary trust provisions contained in a will, pertaining to the care of pets. Probate courts sometimes view such language as "precatory," meaning that the will provisions express what the decedent hopes will happen. So if the Greens, for example, leave their horses to an individual, along with a sum of money to care for the horses, the recipient may not be required to care for the horses or even spend the money on their care.

This happens most often when the will of the decedent violates either a statute or some important matter of public policy. Because our entire legal system, including the probate systems of the states, is essentially a system of balances and counterbalances, the court may not honor the intentions expressed in your will if it violates public policy. This can happen even though courts give great weight to the intentions expressed in a will. A rather dramatic example of a situation in which a court might not honor the terms of a trust created in a will might be a document that left funds and assets to care for a horse, while providing little or nothing for a handicapped child. In a situation such as this, an argument could be made that the testator was not in his or her sound mind, invalidating the entire will.

A more likely problem is the potential for violation of some less well-known principle of law. One example is a legal principle known as the "rule against perpetuities," which no trust is allowed to violate. This rule makes any gift invalid if the gift allows the trust property to be used for longer than 21 years after the death of some relevant "life in being" at the making of the trust provision. Animals don't count as lives in being for purposes of satisfying this rule. Therefore, the only relevant life in being would be that of the testator. So if Mrs. Green writes a will containing a trust provision to care for her horses, the trust will be invalid if it is to last for 30 years, but not if it is written to last for 15 years.

Some states will adopt a wait and see approach. With this approach the court will keep the trust portion of your estate open to see if the animal lives longer than the 21-year limit. If not, then trust funds are properly used for the care of the horse. As you can see, this causes many problems that could have been avoided in the first place, simply by specifying a period of time less than 21 years.

Absent a violation of statute or some principle of public policy, many courts will at least declare that an "honorary trust" exists for the care of the horses. In essence, when a court recognizes an honorary trust, it means that the testator hasn't created a legally enforceable trust, but if the named trustee agrees to care for your horses in the manner specified in the trust, the court will allow this to happen.

BE REALISTIC IN YOUR TRUST TERMS

Even if the Greens establish in their will a trust for the care of their horses that the probate court allows as an honorary trust, they can still run into trouble. Remember the woman Mrs. Green heard about who left her pet groundhog a million dollars in trust? Most people and probably most courts would consider a million dollars excessive. This author has no idea how long a groundhog lives, or how much it would reasonably cost to care for that groundhog for the rest of its life. It would be a pretty safe bet, however, that it's probably a lot less than a million dollars.

At the death of the groundhog, the trust probably specifies that it will terminate and the remainder will go to some person(s) or to one or more entities. It would not be uncommon for a court to allow the estate's executor to set aside some reasonable amount, into the honorary trust, for the care of the groundhog. The court might then order the balance to go directly to the intended remainder beneficiary. The Greens should make sure they take into account the ages and life spans of their horses, and the number of horses, to estimate a reasonable sum to put in trust for the animals' care.

CHOOSE YOUR TRUSTEE CAREFULLY

Even if the probate court allows all the trust provisions to stand, problems can arise with respect to enforcement of the trust provisions. Although the Greens would name a trustee for their testamentary trust, without a human beneficiary of the trust, the horse could have a great deal of difficulty getting the trustee to perform his or her job. If they choose to provide for their horses in this manner, the Greens' should select the trustee of the horses and funds very carefully. Sound legal and financial advice is a must.

YOU COULD EVEN WILL NONBUSINESS HORSES TO SOMEONE

By far, this may be the simplest option. This can be done through a will, without a trust. Preferably, the Greens will also include sufficient funds to care for their horses for the horses' lives. The Greens can make a simple gift of the animals, along with money or proceeds of an insurance policy of which the estate is beneficiary. They should state that they would like the money or proceeds used for the care of the horses, but also give the beneficiary of the horses complete and unrestricted power to decide how to spend the money. In this way, a court is likely to interpret that the will provides for a simple gift, rather than an honorary trust.

The instructions regarding care of the horses impose a moral, but not a legal, obligation on the recipient. (This is an example of precatory language mentioned earlier.) If they do this, the Greens will run the risk, of course, that the recipient of the horses and money may not use the funds in the intended manner. Considering the risks that the Greens might face in having an honorary trust recognized as such, this risk may seem slight, and the process is much simpler.

YOUR BUSINESS MAY OUTLAST YOU

Can the Greens' business continue after their deaths? Yes, unless they've chosen a form of ownership requiring termination of the business at the death of one or both of them. Suppose, for example, the Greens have chosen to operate the horse business as a partnership, with only Peter and Mary as partners. Suppose also that they own the farm as joint tenants with right of survivorship. The partnership agreement specifies that when either of them dies, that person's share of the assets in the partnership will go to the surviving partner. When either of them dies, the partnership terminates. If Mary dies, Peter owns the farm. He must do everything that may be required to wind up the partnership as it had existed, but he now owns the partnership assets and can continue the business.

Even if Peter and Mary both die, it may be possible to carry on the family horse business. If the horse business is placed in a testamentary trust, the court will not look to see if provisions of the trust providing care for the horses are an attempt to establish an honorary trust. If the Greens' horses are a necessary part of their family business operation, provisions in a properly drafted and executed will, with respect to caring for the horses as business assets, are likely to be respected by the court. It will be possible to require someone to care for them, under the terms of the will, at least as long as someone desires to carry on the family business.

It is not necessary to use a testamentary trust to provide for the ongoing operation of the business. The business can simply be left in the will as a gift. If the Greens want to place the business in trust during their lifetimes, they also can do that, using either the revocable or irrevocable trusts described earlier.

DEATH AND TAXES — WE REALLY CAN'T COMPLETELY ESCAPE THEM

At the very beginning, the Greens told us that they want to minimize their tax liabilities. Like most people, they want to pay no more than is required. As the Greens select the form of ownership for their business, they should consider the after-death tax consequences of the decisions they make. They should ask their legal and financial advisers to help them take the fullest advantage of the federal estate and gift tax marital deduction in deciding who does or should own their various assets, and in drafting various estate planning documents. They also should make sure they understand the state inheritance and estate tax rules. With careful planning the Greens can maximize the size of the estate they leave to their children and/or other beneficiaries.

When Peter or Mary dies, the survivor may, or may not, be required to file federal Form 706 to determine the amount of federal estate tax due. The surviving spouse will need to seek professional advice. When the second of them dies, this form will almost certainly have to be filed. Why? By the time of their deaths, the Greens have owned the real property used for the farm and horse business for many years. The business has been successful and the land itself is probably worth considerably more than when the Greens first obtained it. For estate tax purposes, property is usually valued at its fair market value on the date of death. There is an exception for farm and closely held business real property (land, permanently attached structures, and improvements).

Under Section 2032A of the Internal Revenue Code, the executor of the estate could elect to have the real property valued at its farm or business use value, rather than its fair market value. The executor can make this election if he/she satisfies certain filing requirements and:

1. The total value of the property valued under Section 2032A is not decreased from fair market value by more than $175,000 in the special use;

2. The decedent was a U.S. citizen or resident at death;

3. The real property is located in the U.S.;

4. At the decedent's death, the real property was used by the decedent or a family member for farming or in a trade or business, or was rented for such by a surviving spouse or lineal descendant (such as a child or grandchild, including legally adopted children) of the decedent to a family member on a net cash basis;

5. The real property was acquired from or passed from the decedent to an ancestor (such as parent or grandparent), the surviving spouse, a lineal descendant of the decedent, his spouse or parent, or the spouse, widow, or widower of any lineal descendant described above;

6. The real property was owned and used for farming or closely held trade or business by the decedent or a member of the decedent's family during five out of the eight years before the decedent's death;

7. The decedent or a family member materially participated for five out of the eight years before the decedent's death; and

8. The farmland or closely held business real or personal property must account for at least 50% of the adjusted value of the gross estate, and the real property alone must account for at least 25% of the adjusted value of the gross estate.

Let's consider the equine business of the Greens for a moment. If at the death of Mary, the actual fair market value of the business is $800,000, but the special use value is only $400,000, the real property would not satisfy the first requirement and the executor of her estate could not elect special use valuation. If the special use value was $675,000, this requirement would be satisfied.

We already know that they meet the next two requirements, because we know that they are United States citizens
and that their farm is in the Midwest. If the real property was
still used for farming and/or the horse business at Mary's
death, by Mary or her family, the property may qualify as long
as it was used for the farming or horse business for at least five
of the eight years before Mary's death. Of course, she or her
family members must have materially participated in the
farming or horse business for at least five of the eight years
before Mary's death.

Finally, the executor will have to compare the total adjusted value of the farm or horse business to that of the adjusted
gross estate, and the adjusted value of the real property to
that of the adjusted gross estate. The total adjusted value of
the business must be at least 50% of the value of the adjusted
gross estate. If the total adjusted value of the estate is
$1,600,000, the adjusted value of the farm/horse business
must be at least $800,000. In addition, the adjusted value of
the real property alone must be at least $400,000. Mary's ex-
ecutor will probably need the assistance of professionals to
actually make these determinations.

CONCLUSION

It should be obvious by now that, when we talk about
equine law, we really are talking about contract law, tax law,
accounting law, and so forth, as it applies to the specific
equine business. We hope that we have at least made you
aware of some of the potential problems which you, like the
Greens, might find as you plan for your business and your
future. As you can see, decisions you make now can have
impact on your family not only during your life, but after your
death. We hope that you will be able to avoid some of the pitfalls that plague many small equine businesses. Perhaps what
you have read in these pages will assist you in achieving what
is important to you, your family, and your equine business.

RESOURCES

An attorney with expertise in equine issues is the best source of information and guidance, whether horses are your business or your avocation. Finding such an attorney is relatively easy where the horse business makes up a large part of the local economy, but nearly impossible in other areas. Word-of-mouth recommendations — or warnings — are probably your best guide to locating a competent attorney. State and local bar associations also may be able to direct you to an attorney in your area.

Cost might be a factor in your decision to seek professional assistance, and if you are on a limited budget you should tell the attorney. Many attorneys will not charge for an initial consultation, and if you have a simple job that needs to be done, such as a review of a contract, you might be able to negotiate a flat fee rather than an hourly charge.

Finally, use the initial consultation to tell the attorney about your specific problem, but also use the time to learn about the attorney and his or her areas of expertise. Don't be shy! Some states, like Kentucky, generally do not allow an attorney to advertise specialization in a certain field, and it is up to the client to determine if the attorney is qualified to handle the proposed representation. An attorney in general practice who also owns horses probably is a better bet than an attorney with no experience in the business.

If you intend to press into service an attorney with little or no knowledge of horses, or if you want to try and put together a contract yourself (the authors do not recommend this option), you should arm yourself with as much information as possible. One of the best sources of information is *Legal Aspects of Horse Farm Operations*, written by prominent Lexington, Kentucky, attorney James H. Newberry Jr. Available from the University of Kentucky College of Law, Office of Continuing Legal Education, Suite 260, Law Building, Lexington, KY 40506-0048, the book addresses contract issues relating to boarding, standing stallions, foal sharing, and the purchase, sale, and leasing of horses, as well as most other aspects of running a horse business. Aimed primarily at attorneys, the book's coverage is fairly technical.

The University of Kentucky College of Law also publishes the *Equine Law Forms Compendium*, a collection of equine law forms that address most aspects of running a horse business. Forms in the book, which can be obtained from the University of Kentucky at the above address, are intended for reference only, and it must be emphasized — again — that the generic forms almost certainly will not fit the particular circumstances of your horse enterprise. The forms do provide a good starting point for your attorney to draft specific forms for your business, however.

For general information on a variety of legal issues affecting the horse industry, the University of Kentucky College of Law conducts a two-day seminar on equine law every spring in Lexington, Kentucky. Registration information and proceedings books from past sessions can be obtained by contacting the University of Kentucky at the above address.

More accessible to the average horse enthusiast is *The Equine Legal Handbook*, written by attorney Gary Katz. Published by Half Halt Press, Inc., 6416 Burkittsville Road, Middletown, MD 21769, the book contains numerous sample fill-in-the-blanks contracts, which can be adapted to your individual needs. Katz cautions readers that the form contracts in his book are generic and may not cover the circumstances of a particular situation, and he recommends that competent legal counsel review any contract before its execution. This is more than self-serving advice from an attorney seeking another fee. For the same reasons you trust your horse's health to a professional veterinarian, you should seek professional legal advice before signing a contract that might have far-reaching adverse effects on your business.

The *Equine Law & Business Letter* offers on-going coverage of equine law issues. The address is P. O. Box 623, Charlottesville, VA 22902.

A good reference for almost any aspect of the horse business is *The Horse Source*, published annually by *The Horse: Your Guide to Equine Health Care*. The volume includes some 90 categories of services and products, including attorneys conversant with equine law issues. For information, contact *The Horse*, P. O. Box 4680, Lexington, KY 40544-4680.

A fertile source of information about equine law issues is the Internet, and it is beyond the scope of this book to provide a comprehensive listing of reference sites. A few good starting points, however, are:

http://www.horselaw.com — The Web site of Miller, Griffin & Marks, PSC, a Lexington, Kentucky, law firm that concentrates on equine law issues. The site also provides links to numerous other equine-related Internet sites

http://www.thehorse.com — The interactive Web site of *The Horse* magazine

http://www.aaep.org — The Web site of the American Association of Equine Practitioners

TO REITERATE: GET IT IN WRITING

Throughout this entire text, we have told you to write it down. Here is a summary of just a few of the reasons we have given you.

• Write down the complete details of a business plan. You'll be able to compare your accomplishments with your plans.

• Have written contracts and agreements. You'll have a better chance of predicting the outcome, when the unexpected happens.

• Ask your attorney to write the appropriate power of attorney for your needs, so someone else can act for you, when you cannot act for yourself.

• Keep careful written financial and time records. You can avoid paying any more taxes than are absolutely necessary.

• Have written documents to tell others what to do immediately after your death. Make sure they know where to find the documents. Your horses will need to be fed and the stalls mucked, even if you aren't here to do it.

OWNERSHIP OPTIONS AT A GLANCE

Form of ownership	Taxed at entity level?	Participate in management?	No. of owners	Personal Liability?	Duration?	Available in all 50 states?
Sole proprietorship	No	Yes	1	Yes	Life	Yes
C corporation	Yes	Yes	No limit	No	Indefinite	Yes
S corporation	No	Yes	≤ 35[1]	Limited	Indefinite	Yes
General Partnership	No, but does file tax return	Yes	No limit	Yes	Indefinite[2]	Yes
Limited Partnership	No, but does file tax return	Only General Partners Participate	≥ 1 general partner, no limit on # of limited partners	General partners—Yes Limited partners—No	Indefinite[2]	Yes
Limited Liability Company	No, but does file tax return	Yes	No limit	N/A	Indefinite	No
Limited Liability Partnership	No, but does file tax return	Yes	≥ 1 general partner, no limit on # of limited partners	for own actions only	Indefinite[2]	No

1 See text for additional details.
2 Partnership agreement will specify conditions that will cause partnership to terminate.

GLOSSARY

Attractive nuisance — Attractive nuisance is a legal concept addressing a person who maintains, or creates, some condition on his or her property that would be both attractive and dangerous to children. Under such a situation, the property owner has a duty to take reasonable precautions to prevent harm to children who might be attracted to the dangerous condition. Horses in a pasture may, or may not, be considered an attractive nuisance, depending on your state laws.

Agister's lien — An agister is a person who boards horses, or other livestock, for a fee. An agister's lien is the right a farm owner has to retain and sell an animal to recover a board bill following a default by the animal's owner. Requirements for, and the rights arising from, an agister's lien vary from state to state.

Attorney-in-fact — A person who has legal permission to act for another.

Bailee — A bailee is the person to whom personal property is delivered under a contract of bailment. In other words, when you board your horse at another person's farm, the farm owner is the bailee.

Bailment — A temporary delivery of goods or personal property, such as a horse, from one person to another. In a boarding situation, the owner of the horse is the bailor; the owner of the boarding farm is the bailee. The bailee generally is responsible for exercising reasonable care in boarding the animal.

Bailor — A bailor is the party who delivers personal property to another under a contract of bailment. In other words, when you board you horse at another person's farm, you are the bailor.

Choice of law — Contracts generally include a clause stating which state's laws will govern any disputes arising from the contract. A choice of laws clause is most important when the parties are from different states, or countries.

Common law — Rules and principles that arise from general usage over time, or from judicial decisions. Common law principles are different from statutory law, which arises from legislative action.

Consideration — Consideration most often arises in the context of a written or oral contract, and is the inducement to form the contract. When a contract states that, "in consideration of the sum of $ ____, paid by the owner (of the horse) to the operator (of the farm), the operator agrees to board the horse," or something similar, the owner's agreement to pay board and the farm operator's agreement to board the horse are the consideration for the contract. Consideration is a necessary element of a valid and legally binding contract.

Consignment fee — Many sales companies require that the seller pay a fee before the company will accept a horse for sale. This is a consignment fee.

Contract — In its simplest form, a contract is an agreement between parties that creates obligations and responsibilities. In actual practice, a contract includes a variety of clauses and information not directly related to the business transaction. The contract terms should be tailored to the facts and circumstances of the individual business transaction.

Corporation — A corporation is a legal entity created under the authority of a state's laws. The corporation is owned by investor shareholders, who put at risk the amount of their investment, but who generally are not personally liable for debts incurred by the business. Corporations can be one of two types, "C" and "S" corporations, whose differences include tax treatment by the Internal Revenue Service.

Depreciation — When the cost of an asset, such as a race horse or a piece of farm equipment, is spread out over the expected useful life of the asset.

Durable power of attorney — A durable power of attorney is identical to a general power of attorney, except that it remains in force after the principal becomes disabled.

Equine law — Something of a misnomer, equine law refers to the application of a variety of legal disciplines, including contract law, tax law, liability law, and estate planning, to horse owners and horse businesses.

Exculpatory clause — A portion of a contract that releases one of the parties from liability for his or her wrongful acts. A typical exculpatory clause includes language similar to the following: "The farm owner shall not be liable for any injury or damage to the horse, including but not limited to loss by fire, theft, disease, accident, escape, injury, or death. Enforceability of an exculpatory clause depends on a number of factors, including state equine liability laws.

General partnership — An unincorporated business owned by two or more individuals. All partners share profits, losses, and management responsibilities equally.

Hobby loss — A hobby loss is a loss resulting from an avocation (an activity not undertaken for profit) rather than a business, and is not deductible.

Hold harmless clause — A hold harmless clause is a portion of a contract whereby one party releases the other party from liability arising from the contractual relationship. A hold harmless clause in a boarding contract will contain language similar to the following: "The owner (of the horse) shall be solely responsible for all acts and behavior of the horse, and hereby agrees to indemnify and hold the farm owner harmless for all damages sustained or suffered by reason of the boarding of the horse and for any claims or injuries arising out of, or related in any way to, the horse."

Honorary trust — A provision of a will may create an honorary trust, which imposes a non-legal obligation on the named trustee. An honorary trust can be honored by a court if the provision does not violate law or public policy.

Irrevocable trust — An irrevocable trust is established during the lifetime of the maker of the trust, but cannot be altered by the maker. Use of an irrevocable trust may reduce federal estate tax liability.

Lease — A lease is an agreement under which the owner of property (a horse) grants to another person the right to possess and use the property for a pre-determined period of time, in exchange for periodic payments of a specified sum. There is no change of ownership when a horse is leased.

Legal audit — Many attorneys recommend a periodic review of the operation of a farm or business. The purpose is to determine whether contracts are being used, whether contracts need to be revised, whether proper records are being kept, whether local equine liability laws are being followed, whether the bookkeeping is adequate, whether labor laws are being followed, whether insurance coverage is adequate, and to review anything else related to the general legal health of the business. A legal audit is preventive medicine for a business.

Lessee — The party who rents the horse (or other real or personal property) from another person.

Lessor — The owner of the horse (or other property) being leased.

Liability — Liability refers to a person's legal (and sometimes moral or ethical) responsibility for his or her actions. A person who negligently allows another person's property to suffer damage is liable for that damage.

Limited liability company — A business entity available in some, but not all, states, that combines aspects of a partnership (pass-through taxation) and a corporation (limited liability).

Limited liability partnership — A relatively new business entity similar to a general partnership, except that the individual partners are not personally liable for the actions of the other partners. This type of ownership is not recognized in all states.

Limited partnership — An unincorporated business owned by two or more individuals, at least one of whom serves as a general partner and at least one of whom serves as a limited partner. The general partner (or partners) operate the business and are liable personally for the debts of the business. The limited partner (or partners) contribute a specific amount of capital to the business, the amount of which establishes the limit of their personal liability for business debts. The limited partners do not take an active part in the operation of the business.

Limited power of attorney — A limited power of attorney authorizes one person to act on behalf of another only in certain circumstances, or for a specific period of time.

Living will — A document that allows a person to make advance decisions regarding health care that will take effect if and when the person becomes incapacitated. A living will also allows a person to designate another person as his or her health care surrogate, who will have the authority to make medical decisions for the person making the living will.

Passive loss — A passive loss results when an activity in which the taxpayer does not materially participate loses money. The deductibility of passive losses is limited by the Internal Revenue Service.

Power of attorney — Also called a "general power of attorney," a power of attorney is a legal document that authorizes one person to act on behalf of another. A general power of attorney does not continue in force if the principal becomes disabled. (See durable power of attorney, springing power of attorney, and limited power of attorney.)

Revocable trust — Also known as a "living trust," a revocable trust takes effect during the lifetime of the maker of the trust, but can be modified by the maker during his or her lifetime. It helps delay probate, making it useful for some estate planning purposes, but use of a revocable trust will not reduce federal estate tax liability.

Right of survivorship — Right of survivorship refers to the right of one person to the property of another, upon the latter's death. When a couple holds title to property jointly, with right of survivorship, for example, title will pass to the husband upon the wife's death.

Security interest — A security interest is an interest in personal property, such as a horse, that guarantees payment or performance of an obligation. If the boarding farm has obtained a security interest in a horse being boarded at the facility, the farm owner has the right to sell the horse to recover the board bill if the animal's owner defaults. A security interest should be a part of every boarding contract.

Sole proprietorship — A form of business in which a single person owns all the assets of the business, and is liable for all the business debts.

Springing power of attorney — A power of attorney that comes into effect only when the principal becomes disabled.

INDEX

Picture Credits

Anne M. Eberhardt, 49-56; Millcreek, 49.
Tom Hall, 52, 55; Tim Brockhoff, 53.

EDITOR — JACQUELINE DUKE
ASSISTANT EDITOR — JUDY L. MARCHMAN
COVER/BOOK DESIGN — SUZANNE C. DEPP
COVER PHOTOS — ANNE M. EBERHARDT, TOM HALL

About the Authors

Milton C. Toby, J.D., and Karen L. Perch, Ph.D., J.D., are partners in Perch & Toby, a law firm based in Lexington, Kentucky. Toby has enjoyed a lifelong involvement with horses, as an exhibitor of American Saddlebreds; as a competitor in hunter, combined training, and dressage events; as a steward for the American Horse Shows Association; as a director of the Kentucky Horse Council; as a

Milton C. Toby

journalist; and as a photographer. He also is the author of *Col. Sager, Practitioner*, which recounts the experiences of the late Col. Floyd Sager, one of the country's most prominent equine veterinarians.

Perch has extensive experience as a financial planner and counselor, and in estate planning, estate tax, and probate matters. She has authored numerous publications in those areas, and has appeared frequently as a guest on local television and radio programs. She also served on a United States Department of Agriculture-sponsored, multi-state research

Karen L. Perch

project involving farm family finances.

The Horse Health Care Library

Other Titles in The Horse Health Care Library:

- Understanding EPM
- Understanding Equine First Aid
- Understanding the Equine Foot
- Understanding Equine Lameness
- Understanding Equine Nutrition
- Understanding Laminitis
- Understanding the Foal
- Understanding the Broodmare

- Understanding Horse Behavior
- Understanding Basic Horse Care
- Understanding the Older Horse
- Understanding the Stallion
- Understanding Breeding Management
- The New Equine Sports Therapy
- Horse Theft Prevention Handbook

Coming in The Horse Health Care Library:
($14.95 each)

- Understanding the Young Horse
- Understanding the Equine Eye

Videos from The Blood-Horse New Video Collection:
($39.95 each)

- Conformation: How to Buy a Winner
- First Aid for Horses
- Lameness in the Horse

- Owning Thoroughbreds
- Sales Preparation
- Insider's Guide to Buying at Auction